MAY GOD
BLESS YOU AND
MAY YOU ALWAYS
REMAIN RADICALLY
APOSTOLIC IN
WORDS AND DEEDS!

#BILLIONS

RADICALLY APOSTOLIC

The Reality, the Journey, and the Reward of the Call of God!

CHARLES G. ROBINETTE

ISBN 978-1-63903-015-6 (paperback)
ISBN 978-1-63903-017-0 (hardcover)
ISBN 978-1-63903-016-3 (digital)

Christian Faith Publishing, Inc.
832 Park Avenue
Meadville, PA 16335
www.christianfaithpublishing.com

Printed in the United States of America

This first book is dedicated to all apostolic ministers who invested, equipped, encouraged, and believed in the call of God upon our lives. Without the apostles, prophets, evangelists, pastors, and teachers who selflessly mentored us, we would not be ministering, practicing apostolic principles, and experiencing global harvest in this generation.

This book is also dedicated to the three pastoral voices we have been blessed with over the last forty-six years that provided critical apostolic mentoring, encouragement, equipping, training, and correction which together prepared us to thrive through the challenges of the apostolic journey. Special thanks to Pastor William Nix, Pastor Billy Cole, and Pastor Raymond Woodward for your faith in us!

This book is dedicated to my precious wife, Stacey, and my two daughters, Aleia and Brienna, who have joyfully traversed this apostolic way, faithfully, by my side. They never allow me to lose faith in God or people. Though the apostolic process of development often takes place in the shadow of criticism, my girls and my wife always find a way to smile and bear the burden of radically apostolic development with grace. They are my treasures!

Let me also take a moment to thank the Lord for putting it in our hearts to write this book. My wife and I did not grow up in ministry or come from notoriety. The privilege that the Lord has allowed us to be used in His kingdom, to have relationships with His elite apostolic ministers all around the globe, and to be trusted with the apostolic journey that has produced so many powerful experiences which we are honored to share with you in this book, is beyond humbling. We feel so grateful to God to be chosen to traverse this apostolic way! We are filled with gratitude for the call of God upon our lives! We are so honored to be chosen to play just a small role in God's global vision for global harvest! We could never adequately express our gratitude to Jesus Christ, our mighty Savior! We are committed to finishing this race and joyfully laying any crowns or earthly accolades down at His feet in this present world and in the one to come.

CONTENTS

FOREWORD

In every generation, God raises up apostolic voices to challenge His church. Future generations will celebrate them as pioneers of revival and heroes of the faith, but because the challenge is never easy or comfortable, these voices are often perceived to be "radical" in their own time.

The dictionary defines *radical* as "departing markedly from the usual or customary; favoring revolutionary changes in current practices, conditions, or institutions." In today's street lingo, the word *radical* means "excellent" or "wonderful." But the word *radical* is Latin in origin and literally means "going back to the roots or basics; reaching to the center, the foundation, the origin or the principles; going back to the ultimate source." Radical Christianity is root Christianity; it is original Christianity.

To be radically apostolic is not normal in the eyes of the world or in the eyes of the average church member. To be radically apostolic is to have an unquenchable thirst for the supernatural, an unstoppable passion for the kingdom, and an unusual fixation on the biblical principles of sacrifice and submission. To be radically apostolic is to go far beyond what the average person would even dare to live like.

Thankfully, in every generation, God raises up apostolic voices to challenge His church. My friend Charles Robinette is one of those voices for this generation, and this book is his clarion call to live a radical life and see radical results for God's kingdom. You will learn from the elders that mentored him, the experiences that shaped him, and the mistakes that matured him. The book you hold in your hands is filled with firsthand stories, faith-building testimonies, powerful principles, and practical lessons; it is a textbook on revival.

Radically Apostolic isn't just a book that Charles Robinette has written; it is a life that he has lived, with his wonderful wife Stacey and their precious girls at his side. I encourage you to join them on the journey and to become all that God has called you to be.

Raymond Woodward
Pastor
Capital Community Church

In his book, *Salt from My Attic*, John A. Shedd made a powerful statement: "A ship in the harbor is safe, but that's not what ships are built for."

Reverend Charles Robinette left the harbor from the beginning of his ministry and has lived his life in the deep seas of faith and adversity ever since. His book, *Radically Apostolic*, tells a captivating story of fierce storms and astonishing destinations. For the Christian who might be feeling a holy discontent in the harbor, this book will serve as a map for your journey.

Reverend Charles Robinette is a purebred apostolic revivalist. He is renowned across the Pentecostal fellowship as a man of uncommon faith. Miracles, supernatural signs, and Holy Ghost outpourings occur at every meeting or conference he preaches.

It has been my privilege to watch Reverend Robinette's ministry from the beginning. We became friends in Bible school and have stayed close through our different seasons of ministry. In addition, my wife Heather grew up with Charles and his wife Stacey, so we have a special family bond.

I recall when Bro. Robinette was a youth pastor in Ypsilanti, Michigan; he was already a full-blown, unapologetic, apostolic, revival-minded leader. He and Stacey were not mere "pizza and ice-breaker" youth pastors. They led their students into prayer meetings and community evangelism. They experienced exponential growth and many miracles in their youth ministry.

A few years later, Bro. Robinette and I were both in a season of traveling around the country as evangelists. I would regularly call my friend and share the reports of our ministry. "Charles, we had a great revival this weekend. Six people received the Holy Ghost, and eight people were baptized in Jesus's name!"

He would say, "Aaron, that is incredible! I know your ministry was a blessing to that church."

I would inquire, "Well, Charles, how was your weekend? What did God do in your revival?"

He would unpretentiously but confidently reply, "God filled one hundred people with the Holy Ghost."

That's how most of our conversations went while we evangelized. I was always thrilled to hear the reports. I was in awe of the uncommon giftings God had placed in my friend's life. When the Robinette family stayed in our home, I came to understand the power that flowed through Charles's life was not simply the result of his giftings but also consecration, prayer, and fasting.

Eventually our ministries took different paths; I transitioned into pastoral ministry in Wisconsin, and Bro. Robinette's ministry transitioned to both missionary work in Europe and revival crusades around the world. He has become one of the most sought-after ministers in our fellowship.

Bro. Robinette has always been kind to visit our family in Wisconsin and to minister at the local church I am privileged to serve. Every time he ministers, his faith sweeps into the service like a tide, raising all those ships in the harbor and pulling them out into deeper waters. We experience incredible outpourings of the Holy Ghost and miracles.

In his book, *Radically Apostolic*, you will come to know the ministry journey of Charles Robinette. You will read about his formative years, how he became acquainted with revival culture, and the host of leaders who influenced his life. You will also learn that to have apostolic outcomes in your life, you must understand the nonnegotiables: impartation, prayer, submission, humility, and sacrifice. Bro. Robinette masterfully unpacks these core practices and gives us all a path to deeper waters.

One last thing you should know before you read this book. The stories and testimonies will change your life. Each chapter is filled with personal accounts that will powerfully illustrate and illuminate each practice. My faith soared as I read this book. I pray yours will too.

Aaron Soto
Pastor
Apostolic Truth Church

Our experiences and environment shape our perception of the world. My fifty-five years of ministry have been primarily in the United States, where people are consumed with materialism and the cares of life. When thinking about America, I am reminded of the parable of the four types of soils found in Matthew 13. In many cases, the thorns have choked the growth of the twenty-first century Pentecostal Church. I have pastored for fifty years and have watched several a week get the Holy Ghost, while others have fallen away. We see very few signs, wonders, and miracles. The cares of life and the deceitfulness of riches are the primary reasons for this sad reality. Therefore, it is almost impossible for us to relate to a ministry about which you will read. Brother Robinette stretches us all to see the infinite possibilities that come with being radically apostolic.

While on deputation to the United States, we have had the honor to house the Robinette family in North Little Rock, Arkansas, for a few years. Sister Stacey Robinette, Aleia, and Brienna were a blessing to our church and Christian school while here. I can say that there has never been a more sincere, genuine Christian family than the Robinettes. They teach holiness and separation from the world just as passionately as they promote revival. We have been blessed to have Brother Robinette preach for us a number of times in our church and our school assembly, and we have seen many receive the Holy Ghost, their healings, and miracles. I know firsthand from my son, Pastor Nathan Holmes, who was blessed to participate in a crusade with Brother Robinette that God can do miracles en masse. In the twenty-four years of his ministry, I have never seen anything impact him like his crusade experience. He came back rejoicing with the testimony of a great harvest of people receiving the Holy Ghost.

Until you have heard his fervency in prayer, you can never understand his zeal in the pulpit. I can assure you that this family is freely giving their strength and heart to do the work of the Lord. Brother Robinette pours out all of his energy in preaching and harvesting to the point, and he is being spent physically, financially, and emotionally. The Robinette family is genuinely a radically apostolic family.

Bishop Joel N. Holmes
First Pentecostal Church

SPECIAL THANKS

The photo on the cover of this book, which captures the moment when God stopped the rain in Bangladesh and placed a double rainbow over the crusade ground, was taken by one of our dear friends, Sis. Aimee Myers. She and her husband, Rev. David Myers, pastor of Eastwind Pentecostal Church in Palm Bay, FL. They are some of our dearest friends, and we are so thankful that God put them in our lives.

We want to say thank you to all of the ministers of the gospel of Jesus Christ who contributed powerful apostolic testimonies that are included in this book. You are God's elite warriors! It is a high honor and humbling to work alongside each of you in His kingdom.

Thank you to Sis. Denise Johnson for grammar editing this book. What a blessing you have been to me personally from the days when you were my English teacher at Indiana Bible College.

I am very grateful to Rev. and Mrs. Michael Robinson for inspiring me to write a book while we sat together fellowshipping and sharing miracle testimonies following the United Pentecostal Church International (UPCI) Virginia District Camp meeting. Thank you for planting the seed in my heart and spirit. You simplified the process in my mind so that it could be achieved. I love you and your family very much.

Thank you, Pastor Aaron Soto and Pastor Raymond Woodward, for content editing this book. We are so thankful that the Lord gave us the gift of your leadership and friendship. Thank you for protecting us and the kingdom of God through carefully reviewing the words written and even challenging us to prayerfully consider our motives throughout the writing process.

Thank you to the anointed servants of the Lord who translated this book into multiple languages already! Richard Podstatny and Amber Crumbley (German), Melany Murillo (Spanish), Betty Kasidi (French), Rev. Daniel Borges (Portuguese), and Rev. Josh Barsotti and the team in Vietnam (Vietnamese). You are all tremendous gifts of God!

Finally we extend appreciation to all our apostolic friends! What tremendous gifts from God you are! We love you all dearly!

PROLOGUE

*R*adical submission, radical humility, and radical sacrifice will always position you for a *radically apostolic* transformation.

To be radically apostolic means *to be* unreservedly committed to the teachings, doctrine, examples, and actions of the first apostles. It means to live a life that is in total alignment with the first church in the book of Acts!

Where there is a radically apostolic transformation, there will always be radical release of demonstration and power. This will position the church and the world for global harvest!

I believe in global harvest!

As of the writing of this book, there are 7.8 billion people in our world.

It is not the will of God that His church experiences a 10 percent global harvest! It is not the will of God that His church witnesses even a 50 percent global harvest!

According to 2 Peter 3:9, it is not God's will that any should perish.

God's radically apostolic church should have absolute faith that it is the will of God for a complete, 100 percent, multicultural, multilingual, multigenerational, multiethnic, and, yes, even a multiorganizational global harvest!

According to Acts 2:17–18, 21, Joel prophesied about God's vision for global harvest:

> And it shall come to pass in the last days, saith
> God, I will pour out of my Spirit upon all flesh:
> and your sons and your daughters shall prophesy,
> and your young men shall see visions, and your

old men shall dream dreams: And on my servants and on my handmaidens I will pour out in those days of my Spirit; and they shall prophesy: And it shall come to pass, that whosoever shall call on the name of the Lord shall be saved. (Acts 2:17–18, 21 KJV)

God's radically apostolic church must embrace two indisputable facts:

- ❖ Global harvest is the will of God!
- ❖ God is commencing an apostolic shift in His global church right now!

There is no doubt in my mind that a host of apostolic believers are ready for God's end-time plan to reach the whole world. They are ready to play their part in God's global harvest vision!

There is a hunger in the hearts of God's people for the full operation of the fivefold ministry and the gifts of the Spirit released in ministries and churches as never before.

God's people are desperate to see the full demonstration and power of the Spirit of the Lord with their own eyes!

There is a generation of Joshuas and Calebs in our midst who have seen and heard the un-apostolic response of previous generations, and they are pleading with us not to miss this radically apostolic shift moment.

As Elisha was found faithfully plowing in the fields, so are the ministers of this generation.

They have heard the beckoning of the Spirit, and like Elisha, they are slaying the oxen and abandoning the entanglements of this world for a radically apostolic shift. They are readily exchanging positional authority for spiritual authority.

They are sensing the mantles and callings of the fivefold ministry of apostles, prophets, evangelists, pastors, and teachers being released in the Spirit.

If you allow your spiritual ears to be opened, you will hear a Joshua, Caleb, and Elisha generation entreating with the global apostolic church:

> Let us go up at once, and possess it; for we are
> well able to overcome it. (Num. 13:30 KJV)

The radically apostolic church must work as if we believe God can and will give us our entire cities!

The radically apostolic church must have faith that God can and will give us entire nations!

The radically apostolic church must work and have faith that God can and will give us a global harvest!

When Jonathan and his armorbearer went up to battle the Philistines, it was physically impossible for two men to defeat an entire garrison. The Philistines' garrison was a fortified military occupation force. It is estimated that forty thousand troops and six thousand horsemen made up a Philistines' garrison. From a strategy perspective, the plan was suicidal at best. Two against forty-six thousand is not courage; it's crazy! But God loves those kinds of odds. God loves to remove any possibility of anyone stealing His glory. God loves positioning His people to be totally dependent upon Him for their victory.

Take a look at 2 Chronicles 13. Abijah, the king of Judah, the great-grandson of King David, was outnumbered two-to-one when he led his army against the king of Israel, Jeroboam. Can you imagine standing alongside King Abijah and realizing that there were two enemy soldiers ready to fight against each one of your fighting men?

To make matters worse, King Jeroboam also sent troops behind Abijah's army to ambush any of his soldiers that might flee like cowards from the battle! But God loves to allow the enemy to feel secure and overconfident. God also loves it when His people are completely dependent upon Him. In those moments of certain defeat, God does His best work on behalf of His people! When you read the end of the story, your radically apostolic heart should leap for joy:

And when Judah looked back, behold, the battle was before and behind: and they cried unto the Lord, and the priests sounded with the trumpets. Then the men of Judah gave a shout: and as the men of Judah shouted, it came to pass, that God smote Jeroboam and all Israel before Abijah and Judah. And the children of Israel fled before Judah: and God delivered them into their hand. And Abijah and his people slew them with a great slaughter: so there fell down slain of Israel five hundred thousand chosen men. Thus the children of Israel were brought under at that time, and the children of Judah prevailed, because they relied upon the Lord God of their fathers. (2 Chron. 13:14–18 KJV)

Gideon's victory over the Midianites is another example of God's biblical pattern of stripping away our dependency on everything but Him.

I love this passage in Judges 7, when God tells Gideon, "The people that are with thee are too many" (Judg. 7:2).

God tells Gideon, if you take this big army with you, you will say that you did this by your own hand or power. You may assume it was by your own might that you accomplished this great victory. So God instructs Gideon to tell everyone who is fearful to go home. The army that Gideon commanded instantly shrinks by twenty-two thousand soldiers!

If you were Gideon, you would be uncomfortable and probably question whether the career change made sense. You are not a general, not even a soldier, and you do not have any combat training. You lose twenty-two thousand soldiers on your first day as the general of God's army, and you have not even fought a battle yet. With only ten thousand fighting men left, you wipe the sweat from your forehead and move forward. Just when you begin to feel matters will be all right, God speaks again and declares there are still too many people in your army. God tells you to take the fighting men you have left and go down to the water so He can help you send some more people home.

God sends nine thousand seven hundred more fighting men home from the water edge! Now Gideon has lost over thirty thousand soldiers before fighting any battle, and he is left with three hundred men.

Then God says, "By the three hundred men that lapped will I save you, and deliver the Midianites into thine hand" (Judg. 7:7).

This was definitely not what Gideon wanted to hear.

Take note of the size of the army that Gideon and three hundred men are supposed to be facing off against:

> And the Midianites and the Amalekites and all the children of the east lay along in the valley like grasshoppers for multitude; and their camels were without number, as the sand by the seaside for multitude. (Judg. 7:12 KJV)

Do you see the pattern? These are the kind of odds that God likes! These are the odds where the glory and splendor of the King of kings and Lord of lords are on full display!

I love the biblical account of the victory that the Lord gives to Gideon and his three hundred soldiers:

> And the three companies blew the trumpets, and brake the pitchers, and held the lamps in their left hands, and the trumpets in their right hands to blow withal: and they cried, The sword of the Lord, and of Gideon. And they stood every man in his place round about the camp: and all the host ran, and cried, and fled. And the three hundred blew the trumpets, and the Lord set every man's sword against his fellow, even throughout all the host: and the host fled to Bethshittah in Zererath, and to the border of Abelmeholah, unto Tabbath. (Judg. 7:20–22 KJV)

God loves to make a show of His enemies openly!

This realization caused Jonathan to look his armourbearer in the eyes and say,

> Come, and let us go over unto the garrison of these uncircumcised: it may be that the Lord will work for us: for there is no restraint to the Lord to save by many or by few. (1 Sam. 14:6 KJV)

Neither the size of the enemy nor the impossibility of the task caused Jonathan to waver in his faith.

The Bible says,

> And Jonathan climbed up upon his hands and upon his feet, and his armourbearer after him: and they fell before Jonathan; and his armourbearer slew after him. And that first slaughter, which Jonathan and his armourbearer made, was about twenty men, within as it were an half acre of land, which a yoke of oxen might plow. And there was trembling in the host, in the field, and among all the people: the garrison, and the spoilers, they also trembled, and the earth quaked: so it was a very great trembling. (1 Sam. 14:13–15 KJV)

Friends, that is the kind of victory that God wants to give His radically apostolic church in these last days! The earth is going to tremble! The enemy is going to flee before us! Our greatest days are not behind us, and they are not ahead of us either; we are living in the greatest moment of the church right now!

The Lord told me to declare His prophetic word found in Jeremiah 30:16–17 over His radically apostolic church in this last hour:

- All they that devour thee, God will devour them (now!).
- All thine adversaries, every last one of them, God shall send your enemies into captivity (now!).

- All they that have spoiled thee, God will spoil your enemies (now!).
- All that prey upon thee, God will give them for prey to another (now!).
- God will restore health unto you (now!).
- God will heal all of thy wounds (now!).

In 2019, I was asked to minister during the Apostolic Conference in Madison, Mississippi. Parkway Church hosted this meeting, and they focused on being a blessing to North American Missionary families. Pastor Dillon and his family are some of the finest apostolic people in the world; we are very thankful they are our friends.

While in the hotel room preparing to preach, the Lord impressed on me to search how many stadiums there were in the world that could seat over forty thousand people.

A Google™ search for this information revealed that there were at least five hundred stadiums in the world that could seat at least forty thousand people.

At that moment, the Lord gave me a vision of a day when great raindrops of the fire of the Holy Ghost would fall upon every nation of the world at the same time. In the vision, stadiums all around the world were filled with people, their hands were lifted, and tears were streaming down their faces as they were filled with the Holy Ghost, speaking with other tongues all at that same time.

The Lord impressed into my spirit that if we would be radically apostolic, and if we would believe the report of the Lord, we would see those five hundred stadiums filled with at least forty thousand people each. That means, if we have faith for it, if we cast vision for it, if we plan for it, if we give for it, and if we work in unity to see it come to pass, we could see over twenty million people repenting of their sins, being filled with the Holy Ghost and being baptized in Jesus's name!

Aaron Soto is a pastor and a dear friend who is more like a brother to me and one of the greatest kingdom-minded leaders I have ever known.

He shared this tremendous analogy with us during an "Apostolic Family and Marriage Mentoring" session during the United Pentecostal Churches of German-Speaking Nations (UPCGSN) virtual leadership training meeting:

He asked, "Have you ever read the directions on the back of a shampoo bottle? Most directions say, wet hair, apply shampoo, rinse hair, repeat. When it comes to your family and marriage, you can't ever put it on auto-pilot, you must rinse and repeat healthy principles daily."

Bro. Soto will probably be upset with me, but when he shared that analogy with us during the Apostolic Family and Marriage Mentoring session, my mind and heart started to drift a bit, and I began to think about how we could repetitiously implement apostolic principles, faith, and procedure to facilitate God's global harvest vision.

Cast vision, build faith, give sacrificially, build crusade teams, train nationals, secure stadiums, promote effectively, plan accordingly, harvest forty thousand souls, *repeat*! Of course, there are so many more points to consider in planning such a large vision, but could you just close your natural eyes for a moment and allow your spiritual eyes to be opened? Let God give you a spiritual picture of how exciting and awesome it will be when stadiums are filled with His global harvest in your city or nation.

While preaching at the aforementioned, Apostolic Conference to heroic North American Missionaries, the Lord told me He was going to expand the vision of his radically apostolic church. The Lord told me to begin to declare what He revealed in the hotel room prior to the service regarding the stadiums being filled all around the world.

God told me, "Declare to my radically apostolic church who I am awakening even now, I built these stadiums for you! I built these stadiums for my radically apostolic church! I built these stadiums for My global harvest! The global harvest I have planned will not fit in your churches, but from the beginning of time, I prepared venues that you did not build and you did not pay for. These venues will be filled with hungry souls before I return."

God said to me that afternoon, "If you will have faith and speak what I've shown you, you will see it with your own eyes!"

I'll never forget the response of those North American Missions' pastors and wives as they began to hear the global harvest promise of the Lord. Their hearts began to leap. The scales began to fall off their spiritual eyes. Faith began to soar in the building. Pastors began to flood the altars as God gave them visions and faith for stadiums being filled in their cities and nations! God began to give those pastors visions, not for 10 percent of their cities, not for 50 percent of their cities, but God began to give His radically apostolic church faith for a complete global harvest!

Each month, we conduct a one-hour vision, prayer, and planning conference call with the missionaries in Germany, Switzerland, Austria, and Liechtenstein. During these conference calls, I repeatedly tell them:

- Germany has 82.9 million souls. That is God's vision and must be our vision for Germany as well!
- Austria has 8.7 million souls. That is God's vision and must be our vision for Austria!
- Switzerland has 8.4 million souls. That is God's vision and must be our vision for Switzerland!
- Liechtenstein has thirty-seven thousand souls. That is God's vision and must be our vision for Liechtenstein!

One hundred million souls is a large vision, but if we have faith; if we declare it; if we strategically and purposely deploy apostolic training, apostolic team members, and apostolic methods; if we walk in apostolic unity; and if we continue to be radically submitted, radically humbled, and radically sacrificial, God will work together with us, and we will reach the one hundred million souls in the German-speaking nations!

In October 2020, I was in Memphis, TN, with one of our dear friends, Pastor Bill Parkey. We were discussing the global harvest vision and how my family should respond to criticism. Pastor Parkey felt led of the Holy Ghost to call Pastor Brian Kinsey who pastors a great apostolic church in Pensacola, FL. Pastor Kinsey reminded us that Evangelist Billy Cole had a vision to see, in one day, more receive the gift of the Holy Ghost with the evidence of speaking with other tongues than the disciples ever witnessed.

Evangelist Billy Cole said this: "I had to keep saying it until God gave it to me. I had to speak it, not in defiance, not in rebellion against anybody, not against anyone's authority, but I had to say it because that is what God wanted me to have in my ministry. You have to keep saying it, even when you're criticized! They murdered me over saying it, but I kept on saying it until I saw it! You got to say it until you see it! You got to keep saying it until God shows it to you and gives it to you."

I was with Evangelist Billy Cole in Ethiopia when he saw over one hundred thousand people receive the gift of the Holy Ghost in one service.

God gave Billy Cole the vision; he prophetically declared that it would happen, and he saw it with his own eyes!

Pastor Brian Kinsey said, "You got to craft your message before you get in the storm because the storm will always try to get you to change your message."

Prophet T. W. Barnes said, "The enemy is never going to give up trying to take you down. You can't wait until you win every victory to start enjoying your life. You've got to enjoy the battle even when you don't have the victory. If you do make it to heaven, and you hear the pearly gates click behind you, listen carefully because you're going to hear the striking of the arrows as they bounce off the pearly gates because your enemy will never stop attacking until you cross over to the other side."

Without a doubt, there will always be attacks against the vision, but if God has given you a vision for your ministry, city, or nation, no matter how big the vision is, no matter if the vision has never been seen before, prophetically declare it with faith!

Say it until you see it! If God gave you the vision, you are not alone! The same God who gave you the vision will bring it to pass!

The words of Paul have been burning in my heart lately:

> If God be for us [partnership], who can be against us? (Rom. 8:31 KJV)

God's radically apostolic church must understand we are not fighting this war alone! We are in partnership with God! Our God has never lost a battle! Our God has never had a small vision! Our God would never position His people for failure!

> For the Lord your God is he that goeth with you [partnership], to fight for you against your enemies, to save you. (Deut. 20:4 KJV)

> No weapon that is formed against thee shall prosper; and every tongue that shall rise against thee in judgment thou shalt condemn. This is the heritage of the servants of the Lord, and their righteousness is of me, saith the Lord [partnership]. (Isa. 54:17 KJV)

Take a moment to read the next scripture and let it sink into your spiritual system:

> Behold, I give unto you power to tread on serpents and scorpions, and over all the power of the enemy: and nothing shall by any means hurt you. (Luke 10:19 KJV)

Radically apostolic church, we must understand that it is absolutely the plan of God to work with us, in partnership, to facilitate His global harvest vision!

Radically apostolic church, we must expect that God is going to enable, empower, and anoint us to reach all the souls in our cities and nations!

Bro. and Sis. Hulsman are some of our great missionary team members in Switzerland. Bro. Hulsman reached out to me in 2019 and said, "Bro. Robinette, I've got a word from the Lord for you. I was praying about the vision that the Lord has spoken to you about reaching the world, and the Lord told me to tell you this: There will be a sweeping global harvest of nonaffiliated churches. This harvest will open doors into villages, towns, cities, territories, and nations where you have not labored or sown seed." He continued to share, "God said, 'I will give my people land they did not labor in and cities they did not build, and they will eat from vineyards they did not plant!'"

In April 2015, the late prophet, Rev. Eli Hernandez, was with us in Vienna, Austria. He pulled me aside during one of the services and declared this word of prophecy:

> The Lord has sent millions of angels with their swords drawn to fight for you from this point forward! Up to this point, you have worked with one hand on your sword and one hand on the harvesting nets. You have been distracted by the wars waged against you and have missed too much harvest. But not any longer! From this day forward, you will put down your sword and grab the net with both hands, for the harvest will be greater than one hand can hold.

In 1992, I was with Bro. T. W. Barnes. He stopped me in the aisle of his church and said, "Thus saith the Lord, I will give you a harvest. You will see the world ablaze."

These mighty men of God saw a vision of a harvest so big that we, the radically apostolic church, would need both hands to hold the nets! A harvest so big that it would overtake the entire world! A harvest so big that no local church can hold it within their walls. They saw in the Spirit a radically apostolic church experiencing a true global harvest.

These mighty men saw a vision where no one was worried about borders or territory. No one posting signs at their natural borders that say, "No Entry!" No one was worried about position or who was getting the credit.

A radically apostolic church realizes this fact: There is a progressive revelation by God directed to His church of the end-time outpouring of Holy Ghost fire upon the entire world that will produce an unparalleled global harvest.

This book is written with only one motive: to awaken God's radically apostolic church! *It is time to raise our level of expectation!*

Even while you are reading this book, faith is increasing in your spiritual system! Your vision has become blurry, but God is bringing clarity to your vision right now! The spiritual haze of war is lifting, and you can see that God is *for* you!

What you declare today in Jesus's name, you will have it!

What you prophesy into the atmosphere, it will bear fruit!

Make no mistake, it is absolutely the desire of the Lord that everyone in the world repent of their sins!

> The Lord is not slack concerning his promise, as some men count slackness; but is longsuffering to us-ward, not willing that any should perish, but that all should come to repentance. (2 Pet. 3:9 KJV)

> From that time Jesus began to preach, and to say, Repent: for the kingdom of heaven is at hand. (Matt. 4:17 KJV)

Make no mistake, it is absolutely the desire and the longing of the heart of God that everyone in the world is filled with the Holy Ghost with the evidence of speaking with other tongues!

> And these signs shall follow them that believe; In my name shall they cast out devils; they shall speak with new tongues. (Mark 16:17 KJV)

> For the promise is unto you, and to your children, and to all that are afar off, even as many as the Lord our God shall call. (Acts 2:39 KJV)

Make no mistake, it is absolutely the desire and the longing of the heart of God that everyone in the world is baptized in Jesus's name for the remission of their sins!

> Then Peter said unto them, Repent, and be baptized every one of you in the name of Jesus Christ for the remission of sins, and ye shall receive the gift of the Holy Ghost. (Acts 2:38 KJV)

> Therefore we are buried with him by baptism into death: that like as Christ was raised up from the dead by the glory of the Father, even so, we also should walk in newness of life. For if we have been planted together in the likeness of his death, we shall be also in the likeness of his resurrection: Knowing this, that our old man is crucified with him, that the body of sin might be destroyed, that henceforth we should not serve sin. (Rom. 6:4–6 KJV)

I release faith for global harvest into the spiritual system of God's radically apostolic church right now!

You can be certain that God will work for you!

You can be certain that there is no restraint to the Lord!

We know where our help comes from! We know where our strength comes from! We know where our hope comes from! With men, a global harvest is impossible, but the words of Jesus Christ in the scripture below cause my soul to scream, "Yes!":

> With men this is impossible; but with God all things are possible. (Matt. 19:26 KJV)

There is no limit to what God will do in our midst in this hour!

The blind will see, in Jesus's name! The deaf will hear, in Jesus's name! The lame will walk, in Jesus's name! The mute will speak, in Jesus's name! All diseases will be healed, in Jesus's name! The bound will be set free, in Jesus's name! Entire cities and nations will be reached with the gospel, in Jesus's name!

The prophet Haggai declared,

> The glory of this latter house shall be greater than of the former, saith the Lord of hosts: and in this place will I give peace, saith the Lord of hosts. (Hag. 2:9 KJV)

Global harvest is God's vision!

Global harvest is God's plan!

The unprecedented outpouring of the Holy Ghost and power is the promise of God!

Global harvest should be the expectation of God's radically apostolic church in these last days!

Joel prophetically declared these words that belong to God's radically apostolic church:

> Be glad then, ye children of Zion, and rejoice in the Lord your God: for he hath given you the former rain moderately, and he will cause to come down for you the rain, the former rain, and the latter rain in the first month. And the floors shall be full of wheat, and the fats shall overflow with wine and oil. And I will restore to you the years that the locust hath eaten, the cankerworm, and the caterpiller, and the palmerworm, my great army which I sent among you. And ye shall eat in plenty, and be satisfied, and praise the name of the Lord your God, that hath dealt wondrously with you: and my people shall never be ashamed. (Joel 2:23–26 KJV)

Oh, hallelujah, God wants you to understand that He is fully committed to global harvest!

God will pour out His Spirit in these last days upon all flesh!

God is going to let the Holy Ghost rain fall in your city and in your nation in such great measures that the harvest will overflow our church buildings!

God is going to add multitudes to the church daily, and we will not be able to number the increase of the Lord in these last days!

Hear the Word of the Lord for His radically apostolic church— it's time for global harvest!

God is opening the spiritual eyes and unstopping the spiritual ears of His radically apostolic church right now!

God is removing the bit from the spiritual mouth of His radically apostolic church!

A mighty, radically apostolic army of God is going to be awakened all around the world!

We are a conquering army!

Everywhere that God's radically apostolic army sets down its feet, God will give us victory!

We will see the power of God!

We will experience global harvest!

We will declare the Word of the Lord, and we will see an unprecedented increase!

We will see unprecedented miracles!

We will see unprecedented demonstration and power of the Spirit of the Lord!

Jesus said,

> And I say also unto thee, That thou art Peter, and upon this rock I will build my church; and the gates of hell shall not prevail against it. And I will give unto thee the keys of the kingdom of heaven: and whatsoever thou shalt bind on earth shall be bound in heaven: and whatsoever thou shalt loose on earth shall be loosed in heaven. (Matt. 16:18–19 KJV)

If you have been wondering what the future of your church will be in this present world, or if you have been worrying about what the future of your national work will be in all of this global chaos, receive the words of the Lord for His radically apostolic church right now:

> No weapon that is formed against thee shall prosper; and every tongue that shall rise against thee in judgment thou shalt condemn. This is the heritage of the servants of the Lord, and their righteousness is of me, saith the Lord. (Isa. 54:17 KJV)

> But now thus saith the Lord that created thee, O Jacob, and he that formed thee, O Israel, Fear not: for I have redeemed thee, I have called thee by thy name; thou art mine. When thou passest through the waters, I will be with thee; and through the rivers, they shall not overflow thee: when thou walkest through the fire, thou shalt not be burned; neither shall the flame kindle upon thee. (Isa. 43:1–2 KJV)

It's time for us to be radically apostolic so we can see the promised global harvest!

Friends, do not misinterpret delay for denial! Do not allow the intensity of a spiritual battle blur your vision or decrease your faith in this last hour of the church! Do not allow the wounds you received in the house of your brethren to cause you to question your call of God or shrink in your radically apostolic boldness and authority! Do not self-medicate that emotional pain by stepping back and refusing to operate in your radically apostolic calling.

God has compelled me to remind His radically apostolic church that it's time for global harvest, and God is going to use you!

> Ye are of God, little children, and have overcome them: because greater is he that is in you, than he that is in the world. (1 John 4:4 KJV)

God is breathing His vision for global harvest into His radically apostolic church right now! God is imparting radically apostolic gifting into you right now! God is imparting radically apostolic vision into you right now!

In 2 Kings 6, the king of Syria sends a great army to Dothan for Elisha the prophet. Soldiers, horses, and chariots come by night and surround the city where Elisha resides.

The servant of Elisha awakes and sees this great army. The servant of Elisha begins to panic at the sight of this great host that has encamped around them!

The servant of Elisha speaks these fear-riddled words:

> Alas, my master! how shall we do? (2 Kings 6:15 KJV)

Elisha addresses the spiritual problem and releases words of faith to his servant:

> And he answered, Fear not: for they that be with us are more than they that be with them. And Elisha prayed, and said, Lord, I pray thee, open his eyes, that he may see. And the Lord opened the eyes of the young man; and he saw: and, behold, the mountain was full of horses and chariots of fire round about Elisha. (2 Kings 6:16–17 KJV)

Get ready, dear friend; God is about to open your spiritual eyes as you read this book!

We need to hear and embrace the words that Moses declared to the children of Israel:

> And Moses said unto the people, Fear ye not, stand still, and see the salvation of the Lord, which he will shew to you to day: for the Egyptians whom ye have seen to day, ye shall see them again no

more for ever. The Lord shall fight for you, and
ye shall hold your peace. (Exod. 14:13–14 KJV)

Let me declare it one more time to you: God is going to give us a global harvest!

The spiritual fog is about to lift from your life and ministry right now! A fresh anointing is coming upon you right now in Jesus's name!

God is releasing His transformational breath of life into His radically apostolic church, and we will never be the same!

1

RADICAL APOSTOLIC EXPOSURE AND IMPARTATION

You teach what you know…but impart who you are.

—Jack Frost

Impart as much as you can of your spiritual being to those who are on the road with you, and accept as something precious what comes back to you from them.

—Albert Schweitzer

Nothing ever becomes real till it is experienced.

—John Keats

And he returned back from him, and took a yoke of oxen, and slew them, and boiled their flesh with the instruments of the oxen, and gave unto the people, and they did eat. Then he arose, and went after Elijah, and ministered unto him. (1 Kings 19:21 KJV)

He took up also the mantle of Elijah that fell from him, and went back, and stood by the bank of Jordan; And he took the mantle of Elijah that fell from him, and smote the waters, and said, Where is the Lord God of Elijah? and when he also had smitten the waters, they parted hither and thither: and Elisha went over. (2 Kings 2:13–14 KJV)

SETTING THE STAGE

The Word of God is filled with examples of elders intentionally exposing the younger generation to life-shaping experiences as well as imparting skills, insights, and giftings.

Moses was a frustrated leader until he had that critical conversation with Jethro about delegation. Moses, in turn, invested in Joshua by exposing him to the highest levels of leadership and imparting wisdom into his life. Eli was an invaluable gift to Samuel. Samuel brought David in the higher arena of revelation and wisdom.

My favorite example of intentional apostolic exposure and impartation is the example of Elijah's mentoring relationship with Elisha. Elisha had the privilege of receiving apostolic exposure and apostolic impartation from Elijah. That kind of influence was like Miracle-Gro on Elisha's ministry. As a result, Elisha received Elijah's mantel and a double portion of the prophet's ministry.

The sons of the prophets watched from a distance while Elisha poured water on the hands of the man of God. They had every opportunity to be present, to receive, to experience, to be mentored, but they stood back, waited; they observed when they should have positioned themselves for something to fall from heaven or be caught from the prophet Elijah.

What Elisha received could have belonged to them. But while Elisha was pursuing, the sons of the prophets were just observing.

Do not wait for exposure.
Do not stand afar off.
Pursue.

OUR PASTOR

Stacey and I were beyond blessed to have one of the greatest pastors while we were growing up, Rev. William Nix. Our pastor was bold, strong, courageous, and so very apostolic. We *never* did, but many ministers affectionately called him "Wild Bill."

North American Missions' general director, Rev. Scott Sistrunk, documented our pastor's ministerial history with these words:

> In 1967, when William Nix took the church in Ypsilanti, Michigan, God began to move upon him to start a daughter work. He launched his first daughter work in 1970. During the decade of the '70s, the Ypsilanti church experienced tremendous revival and growth. Bro. Nix served as Home Missions director for several years, inspiring the planting of many churches in the Michigan district during this time. He was an innovator in methods of outreach and church growth. In 1982, the Apostolic Faith Church of Ypsilanti moved into a beautiful brand-new campus. After accomplishing this huge task of relocation, God began speaking to Bro. Nix about planting ten churches in the Detroit metro area. This was, at the time, an almost unheard-of concept in the UPCI in North America. There was little or no precedent to follow, and William Nix and the Ypsilanti church would become trailblazers in the church planting movement in North America. During his ministry, William Nix was a successful pastor for many years and served as a district official in many capacities, including

Michigan district superintendent from 1995–2000. For many years, he financed and influenced missionary works in Zimbabwe and South Africa. From his ministry, two fully appointed missionaries, Charles Robinette and Mitch Sayers, are on the field today. However, his enduring legacy is church planting. He is responsible for planting or involved in the planting of twenty churches, of which sixteen are thriving today with an average Sunday attendance of over two thousand.

The churches that our pastor was directly involved in planting are listed below:

- Christian Life Apostolic Ministries, Detroit, MI, Pastor James A. Guerrero
- Jesus es el Rey, Grand Rapids, MI, Pastor Andres Rafael
- Primera Iglesia, Spring Branch, TX, Pastor Manuel Villarreal
- Iglesia Pentecostal Unida, LaFortunita, Honduras, Pastor Leonel Peralta
- Iglesia Vida Cristiana, Detroit, MI, Pastor James A. Guerrero
- Solid Rock Church, Ann Arbor, MI, Pastor Brian Jones
- Solid Rock Church, Lenawee, Clinton, MI, Pastor Tim Richmond
- Solid Rock Church, Monroe, MI, Pastor Tim Richmond
- Solid Rock Church, Brooklyn, MI, Pastor Joseph Romero
- The Rock Church, Plymouth, MI, Pastor Scott Sistrunk
- New Life Church, Garden City, MI, Pastor Chris Smothers
- Life Pentecostals, Livonia, MI, Pastor Anthony Harper
- Solid Rock Church, Dearborn, MI, Pastor Nathan Hayes
- Solid Rock Church, Detroit, MI, Pastor Dale Brooks
- La Iglesia De La Cosecha, Ypsilanti, MI, Pastor Joel Dunning

- The International Church, Romulus, MI, Pastor Art Wilson

God used our pastor in a mighty way to be a catalyst for great local evangelism and unprecedented global harvest.

Our pastor was never insecure about the ministry development of people God placed under his care, even if their ministry development meant that they would leave Ypsilanti, MI, following the call of God to other parts of the world. He never viewed the growth or call of God upon someone's life as a threat to his own ministry. Also, he never viewed their potential departure from the local church as a hindrance to local church growth. He told me once, "If we give God our best, we can be certain that God will give us His best because God will not be a debtor to any man."

Bro. Nix inspired us to be all that we could be for the Lord with these words, "My greatest desire is that you would stand upon my shoulders, see farther than I've seen, and do more than I've done."

There is no doubt about it; our pastor's passion for souls, commitment to global evangelism, and love for planting churches were intentionally imparted into our spiritual system and our ministerial philosophy.

Due to the exposure and impartation received from our pastor, we have embraced the practice of developing the people that God places under our care. We have willingly released those same people to the work of God globally and unbegrudgingly. We have personally and even financially given our best to advance His kingdom, and, without a doubt, we have experienced God's best in return.

BIG IMPARTATION AND EXPOSURE MOMENTS

Our pastor intentionally exposed the saints of the Apostolic Faith Church of Ypsilanti, MI, to the most powerfully anointed apostolic ministries; Rev. Billy Cole, Rev. Lee Stoneking, the late Rev. R. L. Mitchel, Sis. Vesta Mangun, the Guidroz family, Rev. Dennis Lewis, and so many more were often annually ministering in our pulpit. I can still remember those powerful apostolic services as if it was yesterday!

In one of those services in the 1990s, Bro. R. L. Mitchel was ministering when a blind woman was led into the sanctuary. Bro. Mitchel stopped preaching and called the woman to the front. The ushers led her to the altar where Bro. Mitchel met her and told her God was going to immediately restore her sight. Bro. Mitchel prayed, and instantly, God miraculously restored that woman's eyes, and she was filled with the Holy Ghost that evening as well.

During our "Prayer, Faith, and Praise" conferences, there was a crippled man who had been in the church for a long time. I remember seeing Bro. Stoneking coming off the platform and telling that man to get up and be healed. The man got out of his wheelchair and ran around the church, miraculously healed. Sadly, that same man came back around the front of the church, sat back down in the wheelchair, and decided that his medical pension was more valuable than God's miracle. He never walked again.

I still remember when Sis. Vesta Mangun preached about "the Power of Prayer!" Impartation filled the atmosphere, and the entire church was laying all over the floor, lost in intercessory prayer!

There was also a time when Bro. Happy Guidroz ministered, and we had a three-hundred-soul harvest in just three months.

Rev. Dennis Lewis was preaching when my family returned to the church thirty-one years ago. I was fourteen years old when God filled me with the Holy Ghost, and soon thereafter, Rev. Russell Bailey baptized me in Jesus's name.

One of the watershed moments of our apostolic ministry was when Rev. Dennis Lewis was preaching in Ypsilanti in 1991; I was sixteen years old. Bro. Lewis operated with absolute apostolic authority. As Bro. Lewis ministered, the call of God arrested my soul. I could not wait to get to the altar, and once there, I was slain in the Spirit for hours. I could not get up off the floor. Bro. Lewis, my parents, my pastor, and many others lay on the floor with me for a lengthy period of time. Exposure to apostolic ministry had planted apostolic seeds in my spiritual system and would, in due season, produce apostolic calling, apostolic gifting, and apostolic results. That service changed my life forever!

Our church witnessed angelic manifestations, we witnessed the blind receive their sight, we saw the lame walk, cancer was healed, and multitudes were filled with the Holy Ghost and baptized in Jesus's name.

We are so thankful to the Lord for giving us a pastor like Rev. William Nix. There were so many significant apostolic moments of impartation and exposure afforded to my wife and me.

OUR YOUTH PASTOR

Another life-changing apostolic influencer in my life was the result of Pastor Nix hiring a true revivalist as our youth pastor, Rev. Scott Sistrunk. Bro. Sistrunk is the current North American Missions general director for the United Pentecostal Church International. His passion for teaching Bible studies, soul winning, and church planting has shaped our entire fellowship.

Scott and Karla Sistrunk were hired May 1, 1988. My family had just returned to the church. I had never seen anyone pray, dance, and worship the Lord like Bro. Scott Sistrunk. His passion for prayer, praise, and worship was daily exampled and imparted into my life.

Bro. and Sis. Sistrunk loved to teach Bible studies. They were always teaching a home Bible study or searching for a new family to teach to. Their passion for souls was contagious, and it wasn't long before I was infected.

One of my first jobs was to work as a grocery cart retriever and bagger at Meijer on Carpenter Road. I was excited to be filled with the Holy Ghost and be baptized in Jesus's name! After having been exposed to such a passion for souls, I could not be silent. I would spend my lunch breaks teaching Bible studies to my coworkers in the lounge. I cannot remember the exact number of my coworkers who were baptized in Jesus's name and received the Holy Ghost, but during my lunch breaks, we would drive back to the Apostolic Faith Church in Ypsilanti where Bro. Sistrunk would baptize my coworkers in Jesus's name and pray them through to the Holy Ghost. We would quickly return to Meijer before our lunch break was over.

Bro. and Sis. Sistrunk also taught us to never compromise the house of God or our spiritual disciplines for anything or anyone. I remember when my boss at Meijer called me into the office and told me, "You either work on Sunday or find another job."

To me, there was no reason to spend even two seconds considering what I should do. I took off my Meijer jacket and said, "Thank you, sir, but I'm not for sale."

The example, exposure, and impartation of the Sistrunk family had taken root in my spiritual system, and there was no turning back.

Rev. Mitch and Jutta Sayers who serve as UPCI Missionary team members in Germany are the elected general secretary for the GSN (German-Speaking Nations) of the United Pentecostal Church and some of our dearest friends. They are also a product of the apostolic exposure and apostolic impartation of the Sistrunk family.

Bro. Sayers shared this testimony with me:

> After we were literally led by to the Lord to Apostolic Faith Church, we were asked by Scott Sistrunk if we would be interested in a Bible study. We thought, sure, why not? We had never been offered a Bible study, although we had both been involved in Bible studies. We started our Bible studies and heard things we had not heard before from our denominational backgrounds. We both had received the Holy Ghost in Germany but were baptized in the titles. We heard about the oneness of God; the power of the name of Jesus; the covenants of the Old and New Testaments; the tabernacle representation of salvation; the death, burial, and resurrection representation of the New Testament plan of salvation; what it means to be holy; and why this is not just important but essential. There were so many new revelations and so many questions (foremost: Why

had we never heard these things taught before?). While we were receiving this nourishment in our Bible studies, we were experiencing the power of the preached word of God in service, the power of apostolic worship, the blessing of the fivefold ministry that Bishop Nix provided to the church, and we experienced fellowship on a different level than ever before. After about three months of Bible study, we decided to be baptized (rebaptized) in the name of Jesus. Our Bible study continued for about a total of nine months. After this solid foundation, we were able to glean much more from the preached Word. Eventually, we began accompanying others in teaching Bible studies and were asked if we would be willing to teach Bible studies to others. The connections we made then are still intact today, some twenty-five years later.

To Stacey and me (and many others), Rev. Scott and Karla Sistrunk are priceless gifts from God. They have trained, mentored, exposed, and imparted apostolic principles into our spiritual systems. They prepared us for our future in apostolic ministry and apostolic leadership.

Note: As of the writing of this book, God has used Bro. and Sis. Sistrunk to start seven churches in the cities listed below:

- ❖ Ann Arbor, MI, 1996
- ❖ Clinton, MI, 2000
- ❖ Monroc, MI, 2003
- ❖ Detroit, MI, 2005
- ❖ Dearborn, MI, 2007
- ❖ Detroit, MI, 2008
- ❖ Plymouth, MI, 2015

Because of our exposure to apostolic ministry from the beginning of our young and impressionable journey, we were natives to it. It was completely natural for us to incorporate apostolic power and giftings into our ministry efforts.

In 1999, while serving our local church as youth pastors. Our youth group was experiencing tremendous growth. Multitudes of young people were being filled with the Holy Ghost during our youth services and even during "Prayer Club" meetings at local public high schools around our city. Our youth group had outgrown our youth room, and we were holding youth services in the main sanctuary.

During one of our youth services, every young person was running, dancing, and shouting all around the church. An unsaved young couple was driving by the church when they noticed what they thought was natural fire shooting out the doors and front windows of the church. They pulled their vehicle into the fire lane and rushed into the sanctuary to try and save as many people as they could from being consumed by the flames they observed. They came up by the platform in a panic and said, "Sir, we must get everyone out of the building now! They are all on fire!"

I said, "What are you talking about?"

He said, "Can't you see it? There is fire on everyone's head and coming out of their mouth!"

I told him, "Sir, that's the manifestation of the power of the Holy Ghost that is inside of them, and you can have it as well!" They asked if they could run and worship with the young people. I told them, "If you do what we do, you will get what we've got!"

They said, "That's what we want!" They started running, dancing, and praising God with the young people, and both of them were filled with the Holy Ghost, speaking with other tongues! We baptized them in Jesus's name as well.

We are forever indebted to our pastoral leaders for the apostolic exposure to the fivefold ministry and gifts of the Spirit they selflessly shared with us!

As the call of God upon your life develops into active ministry, you can be *taught* ministerial principles and practices. However, when it comes to your apostolic development, there are some elements that must be *caught* through exposure and impartation!

In 1999, one year after leaving active duty from the United States Air Force and becoming youth pastor at my local church, the Lord gave Bro. Billy Cole a dream about a young minister serving as a youth leader in Ypsilanti, Michigan.

In the dream, God told Bro. Billy Cole that I was supposed to be a member of his Ethiopia Crusade team. Thankfully, God also told Bro. Cole that Bro. Nix was supposed to pay my expenses so that I could attend the crusade.

I will never forget the expectancy, anointing, and thankfulness I felt when Bro. Nix called me into his office to inform me what Bro. Billy Cole said. Likewise, I'll never forget the relief I felt when Bro. Nix told me that *he* was paying my expenses!

It was March 5, 2000, when I left Ypsilanti, MI, for Wara, Ethiopia, to join a dynamic group of apostolic crusade team veterans, which included Bro. Billy Cole, Bro. Teklemariam Gezahagne, Bishop and Sis. Stark, Bishop John Putnam, Bro. Doug Klinedinst, Bro. Jim Blackshear, Bro. Steve Willoughby, Bro. Jason Varnum, Bro. Eli Hernandez, Bro. Ken Bulgrin, Bro. Art Hodges III, Bro. E. S. Harper, Bro. Rick Maricelli, Bro. Jathan Maricelli, and so many others!

Ethiopian people traveled from all across the nation to be at that crusade. It was estimated that there were somewhere between three hundred thousand and five hundred thousand Ethiopians present. Standing on the platform, you could not see the back of the crowd. So many people shouting, dancing, praying, repenting, and singing praises to the King of kings and the Lord of lords. I'll never forget when the Holy Ghost fell upon that crowd of people. There was truly a sound from heaven. You could feel the mighty rushing wind. The Holy Ghost fell like fire. When that great crowd of people began to speak with other tongues at the same time, there was a crescendo that sounded like a heavenly symphony! They estimated that at least one hundred thousand people received the Holy Ghost for the very first time during the crusade that day, speaking with other tongues, just like the Bible says.*

There were countless moments of apostolic impartation and exposure during those ten days that it would be impossible to share, but two stand out and left an indelible mark on my ministry.

One of the significant moments of apostolic exposure and impartation was during the crusade team and national leaders' prayer meeting. There was such a visitation of the Holy Ghost. As I'm sure you can imagine, with the caliber of God's people that were in that room, the gifts of the Spirit were in full operation and on full display. I had witnessed small-scale individual manifestations of the gifts of the Spirit in my local church, but I had never witnessed anything like I was experiencing in that leaders' prayer meeting in Ethiopia. The Spirit of the Lord was so strong. The gift of faith was flowing through the room like a tsunami, and diverse tongues, interpretation of tongues, the word of prophecy, words of knowledge, and words of wisdom were arresting veteran crusade-team members. Revelation, anointing, calling, gifting, and understanding were being skillfully released and imparted into everyone present.

I was only twenty-four years old during this first crusade. Nobody on the team knew me, and I did not have stories to share during the team gathering, but those men and women of God were so selfless and intentional about exposing me to apostolic ministry and gifting. I sat silently and listened eagerly as those great heroes of the faith joyfully and freely shared their experiences in apostolic ministry, the pitfalls to avoid along the way, and the pains as well as triumphs experienced on the apostolic ministry journey.

During that first crusade in Ethiopia, I do not think I ever said a word in any of the gatherings. I hungered and thirsted to hear from God through His heroes of the faith. I felt so humbled, blessed, and even undeserving to be in the same room as those great men and women of God.

I will never forget when I first received my UPCI local license. I was driving my pastor, who was the Michigan district superintendent, to our Michigan district ministers' meeting. My pastor said to me, "During this ministers' meeting, if you think you have something to say, *you don't*! Listen and watch the elders. You are too young to have an opinion about things you have never paid any price for or shed any blood to build." I've done my very best as a young minister to never forget those words; to trust my elders, to bite my tongue, to listen rather than speak, and be very cautious before I give my opinion on a matter that I have not shed blood to build.

I have been in many crusades, where heroes of the faith were present at a table sharing. I watched as young insecure men and women of God ran their mouths talking about things they did not know anything about. They missed God-given opportunities to receive apostolic exposure and apostolic impartation. Let's be careful that we're not too busy talking instead of listening.

A word to our young apostolic readers. Approach every exposure and impartation moment with humility, hunger, servanthood, and silence. You should be a sponge ready to absorb everything that is flowing through the voice of apostolic elders to you. Remember, you have nothing to prove and everything to gain.

After an especially powerful service at the Ethiopian crusade, the crusade team returned to our hotel—it wasn't much of a hotel. As we walked up the stairs to our rooms, Bro. Billy Cole shouted out, "Bro. Robinette, you will preach and speak the word of faith at the youth crusade tonight."

I think I actually died when I heard him say that.

I remember telling him, "Oh, I don't have any sermons with me. I'm sure someone else can do it."

He said, "Someone else can do it, but God chose you! You won't need a sermon anyhow. Grab your Bible and go to the crusade. When you walk to the pulpit, God will give you a scripture to read to the crowd and then you will speak the word of faith the way that you saw it today, and it will work!"

Bro. Jason Varnum, Bro. Jathan Maricelli, and I got into the vehicle with Bro. Teklemariam Gezahagne and a few of his ministers, and we drove together to the youth crusade.

There were at least one thousand young people present. I was scared to death! I had never seen anything like this, and I had never done anything like this. I had only seen just a few people receive the Holy Ghost in any one service under my ministry. I thought I was going to throw up.

Bro. Jason Varnum and Bro. Jathan Maricelli both ministered powerfully, and the Holy Ghost was already falling. Then the national leadership called me to come to the pulpit. I still had nothing! No scripture! No sermon! No idea what I was doing! No plan! But as I stepped in the pulpit, my eyes went dark, and I could not see the crowd of young people any longer. In the darkness, I could hear the still small voice of God say, "If you will do what I say to do, and speak when I tell you to speak, I will show you things you have never seen."

Instantly the Lord said, "Read Isaiah 28:11–12 to my people with authority, and I will pour out my Spirit on this gathering of people."

The moment the Lord stopped speaking to me, my vision returned, and I could see the crowd of young people before me. I looked down to open my Bible to Isaiah 28:11–12, and my Bible was already miraculously opened to that passage. It was as if a light from heaven was shining just on those verses. Everything else on the page was a blur.

I shouted these words of God with as much volume, boldness, and authority as I could muster.

> For with stammering lips and another tongue
> will he speak to this people. To whom he said,
> This is the rest wherewith ye may cause the weary
> to rest; and this is the refreshing: yet they would
> not hear. (Isa. 28:11–12 KJV)

I had never felt such authority or power of the Spirit of God before.

I tried to lead the gathering of young people into the outpouring of the Holy Ghost the same way that I saw Bro. Billy Cole and Bro. Doug Klinedinst do just a few hours before. I led the crowd into a prayer of repentance, told them to close their eyes, lift their hands, and begin to praise the Lord. Then I spoke the word of faith, "By the authority of the Word of God, by the power of the name of Jesus, and by the power of the Holy Ghost that is falling right now, receive ye the gift of the Holy Ghost and speak with other tongues in Jesus's name!"

Instantly the power of the Holy Ghost fell upon that gathering of young people, and the nationals reported that over six hundred young people received the Holy Ghost, speaking with other tongues for the very first time.

That apostolic exposure and impartation experience in Ethiopia was a watershed moment for our family and ministry.

Let me share with you one of the more humorous "exposure" experiences during that Ethiopia crusade. There was always extensive communication from veteran crusade-team members regarding what not to eat, what not to do, and what not to drink. We were always instructed to never allow the local water from ice cubes or even the hotel shower water to get into our mouth. They would say, "Just one drop of local water in your mouth and your crusade is over!" After the last crusade service, we returned to our hotel, and I took a shower and brushed my teeth as well. Due to exhaustion, I made the mistake of using the local faucet water to brush my teeth. The local water combined with the excess heat from three days of crusade services while standing in the Ethiopia sun created the perfect storm. Around one hour later, I was hugging the toilet and experiencing many other medical conditions that should never be spoken of in a public setting. Someone called Bro. Billy Cole, and a few moments later, Bro. Billy Cole, Bro. Doug Klinedinst, Bishop Jim Stark, and Bro. Eli Hernandez came up to my room, and all of them squeezed into my bathroom where I was hugging the toilet. Very few things in this life could produce the level of nervousness and personal space violation that I felt when all those heroes of the faith joined me in the bathroom! Then, the very apostolic Rev. Billy Cole spoke, and I could feel the anointing in every authoritative word that was coming out of his mouth! There was no doubt, I was going to be one of the tens of thousands of miracles that happened during the Ethiopia crusade!

Bro. Billy Cole said, "Bro. Robinette, God will heal the sick! God will cause the lame to walk! God will cause the blind to see! God will cause the deaf to hear! God will cause the dead to rise to life again! But…*God will do nothing for the stupid! We told you not to drink the water! Now suffering will teach you!*" He turned around and pushed his way out of the bathroom, quickly followed by Bro. Klinedinst and Bro. Hernandez. That episode was a big "exposure" and impartation moment in my life!

In August 2007, I was invited to join the Malawi Crusade team under the dynamic leadership of Bishop Daniel Garlitz. The Malawi Crusade team was one of the greatest apostolic teams that I have ever been privileged to serve alongside!

The team included incredible apostolic team members: Bro. Charlie Wright, Bishop Greg Hurley, Bro. David Bounds, and Bro. Robert Gordon. These men became like brothers to me. There was a very special bond between all of these team members. No doubt, it was the result of the excellent, anointed, and wise leadership that Bishop Garlitz provided us. There were so many strong personalities and powerful giftings in the core team members of the Malawi A-Team, but Bishop Garlitz was a strong example of radical submission and radical humility. Any pride or arrogance that even tried to raise its ugly head was instantly defeated and decimated.

Bishop Garlitz demonstrated to each one of us two of the greatest weapons there are in the apostolic ministers' arsenal: mutual submission and constant humility!

We watched that giant of an apostolic man, Bishop Garlitz, serve and humble himself before those national ministers and our crusade team. He refused to put himself forward. He believed so strongly in "team" ministry. He would not tolerate anyone who tried to elevate themselves. He would not allow even a hint of pride or arrogance in the team members. And truly, Bishop Garlitz's humble spirit was so contagious that even if there was a moment where pride would try to arrest your heart and soul, the pride would give way to Holy Ghost conviction and repentance.

There were many ministry-changing moments in our pre-crusade team prayer meetings and in our prayer times as we drove to and from the crusade grounds. I remember a moment that changed me as a leader forever.

Following the crusade, we had a fellowship meeting with the crusade team member and national leaders. Unfortunately, there had been many severe problems due to poor administrative planning as well as mismanagement of funds that had been sent in advance to the national leaders.

I watched that humble spiritual giant, Bishop Garlitz, proceed to spiritually correct the national leadership team for their failures in managing God's money and for their failure to administrate the crusade with excellence and care. He never lifted his voice, never spoke down to those men whose failures had hindered the work of God, but rather he started to weep. As tears were running down his face, he proceeded to bare his broken heart before those men of God with humility and compassion. He was disappointed in those men and disappointed in the results. Not because the numbers mattered to him but because the souls of those men and the souls of the nation were being hindered by "little foxes that were spoiling the vines." As he wept before those men, they likewise began to weep and repent.

That humble moment of correction was a catalyst for great change in the leadership team in the nation of Malawi. From that point forward, we witnessed unprecedented outpourings of the Holy Ghost and power!

It would be impossible to document every life-changing moment and every timely apostolic word that shaped our lives, but what you must understand is this: there is no substitute for apostolic exposure and apostolic impartation.

GET IN POSITION

To conclude this chapter, I'm not espousing that you become a carbon copy of someone else. But you must always be humble enough to be teachable and impressionable. Be aware that pride causes people to become a stagnate isolated island. Pride will cause you to spend your life reinventing a wheel that has been rolling for over two thousand years. Our elders are offering us their voice to guide us, their shoulder to stand upon. Let's position ourselves around God's mighty vessels and get in the splash zone of their overflow. Do not stand longingly along the wall waiting for something great from God to fall upon you. Like Elisha, slay the oxen, bury your backup plan and chase after the things that others have chosen to simply observe from afar off. Position yourself to experience apostolic exposure! Position yourself for apostolic impartation!

- Join a crusade team.
- Go on a mission's trip.
- Serve your pastor.
- Pour water on the hands of the prophets, apostles, evangelists, pastors, and teachers that God intentionally places in your life.

Annotation* from the author:

I don't know the exact number of people who received the Holy Ghost during that crusade, but I do know this: it was far greater than what was reported.

Bro. Billy Cole was always adamant about reporting significantly lower numbers to protect the integrity of the report of the Lord.

Bro. Billy Cole always taught our team to be conservative in reporting to avoid the impression of pride, arrogance, or self-promotion.

He told me once, "The North American church is not ready to receive large reports. Even if we cut what God did in half, carnal, jealous, and doubting brothers and sisters will try to undermine every good thing God does."

2

RADICAL PRAYER

Prayer does not change God, but it changes him who prays.

—Soren Kierkegaard

Prayer is the greater work.

—Oswald Chambers

Our prayers may be awkward. Our attempts may be feeble.
But since the power of prayer is in the one who hears it and not
in the one who says it, our prayers do make a difference.

—Max Lucado

> Then they cry unto the Lord in their trouble, and he bringeth them out of their distresses. He maketh the storm a calm, so that the waves thereof are still. Then are they glad because they be quiet; so he bringeth them unto their desired haven. (Ps. 107:28–30)

In the radically apostolic church, prayer comes first.

We must never forget that the inaugural apostolic outpouring was the result of a ten-day prayer meeting. Everything radically apostolic in God's kingdom begins with prayer!

Since the book of Acts, there has never been a great revival without a radically apostolic prayer meeting. There has never been a powerful apostolic saint who did not pray. There has never been a powerful church that did not pray. There has never been manifestation or demonstration of the Spirit which was not initiated by prayer.

When we pray, there is unlimited access to the supernatural power of the Lord Jesus Christ.

In the book, *Prayer Meetings That Made History* (Miller 1955), Basil Miller documents the extraordinary spiritual awakenings of religious groups, cities, and nations. Miller uncovered an incredible common denominator with every awakening: they were all, without exception, born out of fervent prayer meetings.

The twentieth century apostolic revival was born out of a small prayer meeting. In April of 1906, a group of African American Christians gathered together for prayer in a small home on Bonny Brae Street in Los Angeles, California. William Seymour, a holiness preacher, was with them that evening. According to historical accounts, Bro. Seymour's biblical text that evening was Acts 2:4. And they were all filled with the Holy Ghost and began to speak with other tongues, as the Spirit gave them utterance.

That night, a man, Edward S. Lee, and a woman, Jenny Moore, were baptized with the Holy Ghost and began to speak with other tongues. Reflecting on the experience, Sis. Moore said, "It seemed as if a vessel broke within me and water surged up through my being which, when it reached my mouth, came out in a torrent of speech and languages God had given me."

By the end of April, the home was too small for the revival harvest God was giving. The small prayer meeting was moved to 312 Azusa Street. Over one thousand three hundred people gathered in the building and on the streets to experience the power of God!

An eyewitness account of the Azusa Street Revival and prayer meetings states,

As the revival continued for three and one-half years at Azusa, services were held three times a day: morning, afternoon, and night. Tongues-speaking was the central attraction, but the healing of the sick was not far behind. The walls were soon covered with the crutches and canes or those who were miraculously healed. The gift of tongues was soon followed by the gift of interpretation. As time passed Seymour and his followers claimed that all the gifts of the Spirit had been restored to the church. (seeking4truth.com)

Dr. Vinson Synan observed,

Few events have affected modern church history as greatly as the famous Azusa Street Revival of 1900–1909, which ushered into being the world-wide twentieth-century Pentecostal renewal. From this single revival has issued a movement which by 1980 numbers over 50,000,000 classical Pentecostals in uncounted churches and missions in practically every nation of the world. In addition to these Pentecostals, there are untold numbers of charismatics in every denomination who can trace at least part of their spiritual heritage to the Azusa Street meeting. (seeking4truth.com)

Did you catch that? As a result of these radically apostolic revival prayer meetings, there are currently over five hundred million people who can trace their apostolic roots back to those Azusa Street prayer meetings in Los Angeles, California! (Pew Forum: Religion and Public Life [December 19, 2011]; *Global Christianity: A Report on the Size and Distribution of the World's Christian Population* [Archived, July 23, 2013]; seeking4truth.com; wikipedia.org)

The devil is not the primary problem of the church. The primary problem of the church is not worldliness, carnality, or people. The absence of radical prayer is the church's biggest problem!

Think about this: There is no limit and no ceiling on the revival that God wants to give us. Sadly, the church has placed a ceiling of our own making on revival as a result of our prayerlessness.

I doubt that anyone with true faith starts their day with the intention of prayerlessness, but it happens more than anyone wants to admit because of the multitude of distractions in our lives. We must admit that distractions have become very problematic in our personal prayer lives. Netflix, social media, and recreational pursuits have kept many apostolics in the surface level an out of the radically apostolic level of prayer. If we would demote these things and drill down to radical prayer, it would turn our lives, our churches, and our world upside down!

Serving the Lord without a radical prayer life is like going to war without a weapon. Without prayer, you could actually *become* a weapon in the enemy's hands. Yes, the tragedy of prayerless believers is not only the eternal damage they bring upon themselves but rather the damage they perpetrate against other believers and the kingdom of God.

A prayerless father or mother leaves the door of their spiritual home unlocked for the enemy to prey upon their children.

A prayerless apostolic preacher operates without power and authority. His congregation will never see the Spirit of the Lord confirming His Word.

The prayerless leader soon falls into deception of trusting the arm of the flesh and man's wisdom. He or she is soon choked out with pride.

The prayerless church becomes a stagnant pool where bacteria and disease hide. People are given an infection rather than a remedy.

Friends, we must get back to radical prayer! Radical prayer is one of the greatest weapons in the minister's arsenal; it's a weapon the enemy has no answer for.

There is power in prayer!

John Bunyan wrote, "Prayer is a shield to the soul, a sacrifice to God, and a scourge for Satan."

The Word of God informs us in Mark 9:29 that we cast out devils through prayer! In James 5:14 16, we read that the sick are healed through prayer! In Acts 9:40 we see evidence that the dead are raised through prayer!

The apostle Paul wrote these words:

> For though we walk in the flesh, we do not war after the flesh: (For the weapons of our warfare are not carnal, but mighty through God to the pulling down of strong holds;) Casting down imaginations, and every high thing that exalteth itself against the knowledge of God, and bringing into captivity every thought to the obedience of Christ. (2 Cor. 10:3–5 KJV)

Jesus had a lot to say about prayer:

> Ask, and it shall be given you; seek, and ye shall find; knock, and it shall be opened unto you. (Matt. 7:7 KJV)

> And all things, whatsoever ye shall ask in prayer, believing, ye shall receive. (Matt. 21:22 KJV)

> Therefore I say unto you, What things soever ye desire, when ye pray, believe that ye receive them, and ye shall have them. (Mark 11:24 KJV)

> And whatsoever ye shall ask in my name, that will I do, that the Father may be glorified in the

Son. If ye shall ask any thing in my name, I will
do it. (John 14:13–14 KJV)

If we are going to be the global apostolic influencers that God
has called us to be in these last days, we must enter into the realm
of radical prayer and radically apostolic prayer meetings. Radically
apostolic prayer will give way to the radically apostolic power and
demonstration of the Spirit.

In 1 Samuel, when Hannah prayed, her womb opened up, and
she began to bear children!

The womb of the church opens through prayer; the church
conceives as a result of prayer. Without prayer, the church will be
barren and unfruitful; it will have a form of godliness but lacking
power and apostolic authority. With prayer, however, God's church
will become an unstoppable force.

I think of First Pentecostal Church in North Little Rock,
Arkansas, led by Bishop Joel Holmes and Pastor Nathan Holmes.
They have always said, "This church was built on prayer!"

Decades of fervent, faithful, and radical prayer has broken the
back of the devil in North Little Rock, AR, and God continues to
give them local favor and global apostolic influence in His kingdom!

I also think of the Pentecostals of Alexandria, Alexandria, LA,
led by powerful, global apostolic influencers: the late Rev. G. A.
Mangun, Rev. Anthony Mangun, and Rev. Gentry Mangun.

Their twenty-four-hour prayer focus is legendary. They have
spent decades teaching their church and our entire fellowship how
to pray "through" the tabernacle. As a result, Alexandria is exploding
with apostolic revival and the demonstration and power of the Holy
Ghost! God has given them local favor and global apostolic influence
in His kingdom!

OUR EXPERIENCES WITH PRAYER

There is absolutely nothing that radically apostolic prayer cannot do!

In 2001, my wife and I were evangelizing and witnessed over four thousand people with the Holy Ghost. During the UPCI General Conference in Louisville, KY, Missionary and Sis. Ciulla invited us to be their furlough replacements in Belgium while deputized in the United States. We immediately submitted the opportunity to our pastor, Rev. William Nix. After a season of prayer, our pastor confirmed that it was the will of God for us to accept our first Associate in Missions (AIM) trip. We sold our house, our car, and most of our belongings and prepared to leave for the nation of Belgium on February 2, 2002.

As we continued our travels before our departure for the mission field, God continued to give us an unprecedented outpouring of His Spirit across North America.

During one of our last North American services in February 2002, prior to leaving for Belgium, a well-meaning pastor came to us and said, "Bro. and Sis. Robinette, God is giving you great favor and a great harvest in North America. Belgium and all of Europe are burnt over and can never have the kind of harvest you are seeing here. If you go to Europe, it and the missionary team will kill you and your ministry! Please cancel your AIM application and stay an evangelist."

As you can imagine, the words from that elder really shook us up. We were still very young; I was twenty-seven years old, and Stacey was twenty-six. We brought the counsel of that pastor to the throne of God. God's response was resounding: "If you will go, I will confirm my word. People are waiting for you now."

We packed our bags and left for Belgium with complete confidence in God's word.

We arrived in Brussels, Belgium, February 3, 2002. On that very day, we received a phone call at the church. It was an African woman. She said, "Is this Charles Robinette? We have been waiting for you. We have a group of people who have been studying the Word of God, and we want to know about the Holy Ghost and water baptism in Jesus's name."

Someone was dispatched to us to bring us back to a tiny apartment packed with twenty people seated in chairs, on the floor, and every conceivable space. We taught them the one-hour Bible study,

Into His Marvelous Light™. While we yet spoke the Word, people began to fall on the floor speaking with other tongues as the Spirit gave them utterance. Many came back to the church with us to be baptized in Jesus's name. We later asked that woman how she knew my name. She said, "I was in prayer when the Lord told me to dial a phone number I was not familiar with and ask for a preacher named Charles Robinette who I had never met. The Lord told me that that this man would tell me what I should do."

There is nothing that prayer cannot do!

In 2018, Pastor Pajo, an independent apostolic preacher in Liege, Belgium, contacted me. During our communications, he told me that their church was in ten days of prayer and fasting. They were specifically asking the Lord to pour out the gift of the Holy Ghost upon their congregation. He requested that I come and preach for his congregation.

My wife and I traveled to the city of Liege, Belgium, on October 27, 2018. When we entered the sanctuary, there were hundreds of people raptured in radically apostolic prayer. They were calling upon the Lord for an outpouring of the Spirit of God.

A woman, by the name of Betty, was asked to translate for me into the French language. She once worked as a translator for the European Commission and several other European associations that reported to the European Commission. Betty was not a member of the church. Of all the translators I have worked with through the years, she was one of the best.

While I was preaching, the Spirit of the Lord was overwhelming Betty. While she was translating, she was trembling under the power of the Holy Ghost. When the word of faith was spoken, Betty crumpled to the floor speaking with other tongues! In that same Sunday morning service, about 143 people were filled with the gift of the Holy Ghost, 115 testified of notable miracles, and many said they wanted to be baptized in the name of Jesus!

Radically apostolic prayer paved the way for this incredible outcome.

The following year, May 2019, Bishop Jim Stark (district superintendent of the Ohio UPCI) and Rev. Marvin Walker (pastor in

Michigan UPCI District) spent ten days training Pastor Pajo's congregation in our fundamental apostolic doctrine and our biblical apostolic identity. When they concluded their weeklong training through Apostolic Ministry Training Center (AMTC), Bro. Walker and Bishop Stark reported that eighty to ninety trinitarians, including the translator, received the revelation of the oneness of God. Also, forty-eight were filled with the Holy Ghost with the evidence of speaking in other tongues, and sixty were baptized in the name of Jesus!

Later in 2019, one of our dearest friends and an irreplaceable gift from God to our family during one of the most difficult seasons of our ministry, Pastor Jim Blackshear (North American Missions director and presbyter for Alaska), took a team from Anchorage, Alaska, to continue AMTC training with the independent Liege, Belgium, church. God used the Alaska team in a mighty way, and sixty people were baptized in Jesus's name in one service! Many more were filled with the Holy Ghost during those services as well!

It was not a program, mass evangelism, or any personalities that gave birth to this great Holy Ghost awakening in Belgium. It was fervent, radically apostolic prayer. It will always be a fervent, radically apostolic prayer that shakes the nations!

We are continuing AMTC training with this great church, and we are expecting a mighty breakthrough in the nation of Belgium.

WHAT IS RADICALLY APOSTOLIC PRAYER?

Radically apostolic prayer is unscripted. It isn't pretty prayer. It's not professional prayer. It's not crowd-pleasing prayer. It's not eloquent prayer. Radically apostolic prayer is God-inspired prayer that will undoubtedly move mountains and dispatch heavenly forces to engage in strategic kingdom spiritual warfare.

Radically apostolic prayer seeds the natural and spiritual atmosphere with the creative power of God's spoken word and Spirit. It shakes the foundations of prisons. It releases the shackles from the hands and feet of God's people. It fully engages principalities, powers, and rulers of the darkness of this world and defeats them. It often involves being carried away into the Spirit where you begin to see the situation from God's vantage point.

When I personally engage in radically apostolic prayer, it involves praying in tongues authoritatively for people and nations until I feel the spiritual release that God's divine objective has been achieved in the situation. It involves authoritative speaking, declaring and prophesying that which is not, as if it already happened.

In 1994, we were stationed at the USAF base in Ramstein, Germany. Almost immediately upon arrival, my wife became very sick. She was in a constant state of fever and developed excruciatingly painful red bumps all over her body. Although we visited several recommended doctors and specialists, none could find the source of the problem or provide her any kind of relief.

After returning to base housing following an appointment at the Landstuhl Regional Medical Center, my wife, wracked with pain, laid down on the floor in the middle of the entryway of our apartment and cried. I felt completely helpless; I had no idea how to help her. The Lord clearly spoke to me and said, "Take your Bible, lay it upon your wife's body, and with authority declare my promises of healing and miracles over her boldly, and I will heal her!"

I immediately did what God said. I prayed the word of God with boldness and authority. What the local doctors could not find, what the specialist could not resolve, and what medicine could not cure, God miraculously and instantaneously accomplished! My wife's temperature returned to normal, the red bumps on her skin disappeared before our eyes, and whatever the source of the problem was, it didn't matter because it never returned!

In 2003, I was invited by my dear friend, Missionary Joe Cooney, to minister in Dublin. When Bro. Cooney dropped me off at the hotel, I collected my key from the front desk and proceeded to my assigned room. When I opened the door to the hotel room and walked inside, fear instantly gripped my heart. The hair on my arms and on the back of my neck stood up straight. Somebody or something was in my room waiting on me.

When I turned on the light, a demonic spirit was standing by the bed. Although it was wearing apparel that I can only describe as utterly black, its face was visible and filled with rage. Without touching the floor, the demonic spirit moved across the room and physically pushed me against the wall. With a voice full of the pure venom of hate, the spirit snarled, "I am the prince of this city, and you are nothing! I was here before you, and I will be here after you! If you don't leave now, I will kill you!"

While I stared that demonic spirit in the eye, something quickened inside of me. I began to pray in that authoritative Holy Ghost tongue, radical prayer. The grip the demonic spirit had upon my chest began to loosen. I could see in the eyes of that spirit that whatever authority it was trying to convince me it possessed over me, it was a false authority and was beginning to waver.

An inferno of righteous indignation exploded in me, and I shouted in the face of that demonic spirit, "You may have been here before me, but I know somebody who was here before you!"

I proceeded to quote John 1:1–5, 14 boldly and with authority against that demonic spirit.

> In the beginning was the Word, and the Word was with God, and the Word was God. The same was in the beginning with God. All things were made by him; and without him was not any thing made that was made. In him was life; and the life was the light of men. And the light shineth in darkness; and the darkness comprehended it not. And the Word was made flesh, and dwelt among us (and we beheld his glory, the glory as of the only begotten of the Father,) full of grace and truth. (John 1:1–5, 14 KJV)

The demonic spirit began to tremble with fear! It released its grip on my chest. It started bouncing like a pinball from one side of the room to the other until it finally bounced out of the window of the hotel!

Rather than be pushed into a corner by the enemy, I responded with radical prayer. Not surprisingly, there was a great breakthrough during the services we had that weekend in Dublin, Ireland. People received the Holy Ghost, were baptized in Jesus's name. That demonic spirit never showed its face to me again.

FIVE ELEMENTS OF RADICALLY APOSTOLIC PRAYER

Prayer that manifests demonstration and power of the Spirit is what I would describe as radically apostolic prayer. Five elements are needed to activate radically apostolic prayer.

Element 1: Agreement

Jesus said,

> Again I say unto you, That if two of you shall agree on earth as touching any thing that they shall ask, it shall be done for them of my Father which is in heaven. For where two or three are gathered together in my name, there am I in the midst of them. (Matt. 18:19–20 KJV)

It was agreement prayer in Acts 1:14 that gave birth to the unprecedented apostolic outpouring in Acts 2!

Luke records a prayer meeting in Acts 4:31. The results were astounding. The place was shaken. They were all filled with the Holy Ghost. They spoke the Word of God with boldness.

In verse 32, Luke stated, "And the multitude of them that believed were of *one* heart and of *one* soul." Agreement is powerful!

In 1993, at eighteen years old and backslidden from the church, I joined the United States Air Force. My initial Air Force Special Codes (AFSC) was 568th Security Forces Squadron (SFS) or Military Police. I spent six weeks in basic training in San Antonio, Texas, and then I spent another four weeks in Security Forces Police Academy (also in San Antonio, Texas). Following those trainings, I spent two more months being trained by the Army in Fort Dix, New Jersey, to provide air base ground defense.

At the end of my initial training, I was scheduled to be deployed with my unit to a remote base in Turkey for a one-year duty assignment. At that time, my mother, Lavonda Robinette, was strong in the church and a powerful prayer warrior. Without consulting the USAF and asking how her prayers might affect military readiness, she decided to change my orders through radical prayer. During a women's prayer meeting, she put a map on the floor, and the ladies began to fervently, radically pray that God would change my orders.

At the same time my mom was praying, my unit was at the airport waiting to depart for the Middle East when a captain came running down the terminal hallway and said, "Robinette, I've never seen this before, but you are not being deployed with your unit. You've been cut new orders, and you are going to Germany."

I switched flights and took off for Frankfurt, Germany.

The wise Solomon observed,

> Two are better than one; because they have a
> good reward for their labour. (Eccles. 4:9 KJV)

Two are better than one! This why being part of a local church is so important! When you have a church family, you are not alone! You have brothers and sisters to pray in agreement and to bear on another's burdens.

Our spiritual impact is multiplied when we have someone go to battle with us.

The Lord told the Hebrews,

> And ye shall chase your enemies, and they shall
> fall before you by the sword. And five of you shall
> chase an hundred, and an hundred of you shall
> put ten thousand to flight: and your enemies shall
> fall before you by the sword. (Lev. 26:7–8 KJV)

In 1994, the Military Ministry's coordinator was Missionary Arlie Enis. He was in prayer when the Lord directed him to go to the Frankfurt airport and wait on a young man named Charles Robinette.

I was waiting for my luggage in baggage claim when Bro. Enis tapped me on the shoulder and said, "Are you Charles Robinette?"

I didn't know who he was, but I simply said, "Yes, sir."

Bro. Enis looked me directly in the eyes and said, "I heard you are running from God, and I am here to slow you down! Get in my car and I will take you back to my church and pray you back through to the Holy Ghost."

Without hesitation, I got in the car with this bold apostolic UPCI missionary that I did not know and traveled back to Landstuhl, Germany, with him. He took me to his church, to the altar, and prayed me back through to the Holy Ghost.

I was a spiritually isolated soul, but a simple prayer meeting with brotherly agreement shattered the enemy's work in my life.

There is always breakthrough, transformation, and intervention when God's people agree in radical prayer!

If you have a lost loved one, if you're going through a great trial, if you need an answer from God, unify with someone in fervent prayer.

Element 2: Righteousness

> The effectual fervent prayer of a righteous man availeth much. (Jas. 5:16 KJV)

Righteousness is God's priority for his people. It is a nonnegotiable prerequisite for Him to hear us and heal us. If you want to enter into the realm of radical prayer, you must evict sin from your life.

The Lord told Solomon,

> If my people, which are called by my name, shall humble themselves, and pray, and seek my face, and turn from their wicked ways; then will I hear from heaven, and will forgive their sin, and will heal their land. Now mine eyes shall be open, and

mine ears attent unto the prayer that is made in
this place. (2 Chron. 7:14–15 KJV)

A believer who is living in sin and not separated from the world
will not know the true power of prayer. But a righteous person can
literally change the world through prayer. A righteous person has permission to make great requests of God and will witness great power.

Aleia, our oldest daughter, was born when we were on deputation in Michigan. One weekend, I left my family in Ypsilanti,
Michigan, to minister in southern Illinois. Our Sunday night service
was filled with the miraculous! Multitudes were filled with the Holy
Ghost, baptized in Jesus's name, and so many testified of notable
miracles.

Following the service, I joined about twenty of the leaders
from the church at a restaurant. We were sitting around a large table
recounting and rejoicing together over the great things that the Lord
had done. I did not have cellular service in that town, so I left my
cell phone at the hotel. While we all fellowshipped, the pastor's cell
phone began to ring. The atmosphere changed quickly when the pastor answered the phone. He said, "Yes, sir, he's here. Jesus! Yes, I will
have him call his family."

Tears were already streaming down the pastor's face when he
looked at me and said, "Bro. Robinette, I'm so sorry to tell you this,
but your daughter, Aleia, has died. Your pastor and your family are
all trying to reach you."

I could hear and feel the pounding of my heart in my ears. My
throat began to close, and I could not breathe. Shock set in, and I did
not say a word. I just sat there trying to understand the words that
were spoken to me that seemed impossible to process.

People began to weep all around the table. Ministers' wives
sobbed as they all awaited my response to the news.

I didn't know how long I sat there unresponsive, but at some
point, the pastor put his hand on my arm and said, "Bro. Robinette,
did you hear what I said? Do you understand?"

I said, "Yes, sir."

Tears were spilling down my face as I stood up from the table. As I stood, everyone at the table stood with me. I lifted my hands, turned my tear-stained face toward heaven, and shouted, "Jesus, she was yours long before she was ever mine. If it serves your kingdom's purpose, you can have her, and I'll never complain, but if you don't mind, I'd like for you to give her back to me!"

Although it was late, I had an overwhelming desire to get back to Michigan to be with my wife and hold my baby. I grabbed my car keys and started to leave. The pastor begged me not to drive, but I simply could not stay.

While driving, I finally reached a place where I had a phone signal. My wife called me weeping. Aleia had experienced a febrile seizure in her crib, vomited, and had choked in her crib without my wife's knowledge. When my wife found her, she was already blue from lack of oxygen. She immediately cleared her airways and called emergency services. While she waited, she cradled Aleia in her arms and called on the name of the Lord. Aleia's heart began to beat again.

Upon their arrival, the emergency workers immediately went to work on my precious daughter. The responders told my wife that Aleia would not survive the night, that she should gather our family together. Aleia's heart stopped three times that night.

I was driving well over one hundred miles per hour to get to my wife and daughter when my phone rang unexpectedly. It was Rev. Billy Cole.

I answered the phone, and before I spoke a word, Bro. Billy Cole said, "Bro. Robinette, slow down and drive the speed limit. The Lord has heard your prayer. Aleia will live and not die!"

Bro. Cole proceeded to pray in tongues with great authority for a lengthy period of time. Then my phone rang again. It was my wife! She said, "Baby, the doctors are in shock! All Aleia's vital signs just stabilized, and she sat up and asked for two things: her daddy and purple popsicle!"

Of course, I still drove very fast and made it to Michigan in record time.

There is no question in my mind that the turning point was the fervent prayer of a righteous man who had power with God. God never ignores the radical prayers of His righteous!

When you righteously align yourself with God, there are no limitations!

> If ye abide in me, and my words abide in you, ye
> shall ask what ye will, and it shall be done unto
> you. (John 15:7 KJV)

In 2013, my precious wife, Stacey Robinette, received a notable miracle of healing, and she was able to share this now-viral testimony for the first time during a service with Pastor Anthony Mangun at the Pentecostals of Alexandria on September 17, 2018:

*****

As appointed missionaries to Germany, Switzerland, Austria, and Liechtenstein, we completed our deputation and were returning to the field. I was tired and losing weight rapidly. I thought it was normal considering the pressure we were under with all the preparation that is required for a missionary to transition from deputation to the field and vice versa.

Three weeks before returning to Vienna, Austria, as I put my seat belt on, I felt a lump on my neck. Immediately we made an appointment to see a doctor, who scheduled x-rays and blood work.

The results that came back caused major concern for our family and our missions' appointment. The x-rays showed cancerous spots on my lungs, neck, and in other areas of my body.

The doctor told us, "You have cancer throughout the whole left side of your body."

I remember thinking within myself that day, *God, surely cancer is not part of the process to get our family to the place you promised?*

While I probably should have done other things, it seemed appropriate to drive to Starbucks and get my favorite drink, a double-shot espresso with steamed half-and-half and one Splenda. I even drove myself to get a pedicure as well!

I sat there in that parking lot with no tears, no feelings, just emptiness, sudden brokenness, and silence. My question was, "What does this mean, God?" I told the Lord, "We don't have time for cancer. I have a husband and two young daughters to care for. We are leaving for Austria to serve You, and this does not fit our plan."

As I sat there, God reminded me of my favorite scripture passage:

> But now thus saith the Lord that created thee, O Jacob, and he that formed thee, O Israel, Fear not: for I have redeemed thee, I have called thee by thy name; thou art mine. When thou passest through the waters, I will be with thee; and through the rivers, they shall not overflow thee: when thou walkest through the fire, thou shalt not be burned; neither shall the flame kindle upon thee. (Isa. 43:1–2 KJV)

More tests were scheduled. As my husband and I waited in the lobby, I told my husband, "This doesn't matter. No matter what happens, we go to the field and serve the Lord."

We spoke no other words. At some point, the doctor called out my name. I turned and hugged my husband. I lay in a round x-ray unit, and everything was silent but the pounding of my heart.

I told the Lord, "God I'm afraid. I don't know what do."

I had no other words. I could hardly swallow. Everything around me was silent. Then as my eyes fill with tears, I just began to worship the Lord. Tears were falling from my cheeks as I thanked Him.

The test came back and confirmed the results from the previous doctor, but we decided we were not going to believe the report of the doctors. We began to claim the promises of God over my body. We prophesied that this would not be my end, that my body would be completely healed.

When we came back home that evening, we received a phone call from Bro. Cunningham, Bro. Gleason, and Bro. Stoneking. They prayed the prayer of faith over my body. Bro. Stoneking said, "The Lord has healed you, go get tested again."

We went back again and tests were run again. We waited for the results from the final test; it was the longest waiting season of our lives.

I could still feel the lump in my neck, but after a few days, the other lumps that were present began to decrease in size. We knew God was healing my body. A few days later the call came from the doctor. He said, "We cannot explain what has happened to you. When you came in for the tests, all the exams, all the blood work, and all the screenings were clear: you had cancer throughout your whole body, but after your final tests finished, we cannot find one trace of cancer in your body at all!"

I am cancer-free! God is faithful to his promise!

*****

If you walk with God, God will walk with you! If you are faithful to God, God will be faithful to you! The radical prayer of a righteous man has unlimited radically apostolic power!

Element 3: Fervency

Paul sends a greeting from a little known figure of the early church, Epaphras. Little known to us but well known by heaven and a hero of the faith.

> Epaphras, who is one of you, a servant of Christ, saluteth you, always labouring fervently for you in prayers, that ye may stand perfect and complete in all the will of God. (Col. 4:12 KJV)

What an incredible description of a great man! Epaphras was always laboring fervently in prayer for the saints.

The word, *fervent* means intense, hot, glowing, burning. Fervent prayer speaks of fire, passion, and anointing!

Have you ever witnessed someone praying like that? When you see someone praying fervently, you can tell they believe in what they are praying.

Fervency is the difference between routine and radical praying.

I again call your attention to the words of James, the pastor of the church of Jerusalem:

> The effectual *fervent* prayer of a righteous man availeth much. (Jas. 5:16 KJV)

Fervent prayers of the righteous are effective; they get the job done. When you begin to pray fervently, something is going to happen!

In chapter 6, Bishop Jim Stark shares our personal testimony about the miracle protection of God while we were ministering in Sheikhupura, Pakistan. Let me tell you about the fervent prayer that gave birth to that miracle.

My wife Stacey and daughters were in North Little Rock, AR, at the First Pentecostal Church when I sent her a text message from Sheikhupura asking her to cover our team in prayer immediately. I did not provide her any of the details because I did not want to cause her to worry, but she knew the situation was serious. She went into the sanctuary and began to fervently call upon the Lord. While in the moment of fervent prayer, the Lord gave her a vision and a word for our team. She saw the Lord dispatching thousands of mighty warring angels that were quickly descending from heaven to Sheikhupura, Pakistan, and those angels were surrounding our team with their swords drawn, and there were many rows of angels around us. Then the Lord spoke to her and said, "Tell my ministers what you have seen and tell them that I will make them invisible to their enemies!"

Bishop Stark tells the rest of the testimony from his perspective in chapter 6, but there were many churches, including Calvary in Columbus, FPC in Little Rock, POA in Alexandria, and Parkway Church in Madison that went into immediate fervent prayer that produced miraculous protection for God's people.

Pastor Jason Dillon sent this prophetic word during their fervent prayer meeting: "In the name of Jesus! I declare the piercing power of God to prevail in Pakistan even now! We speak into the very atmosphere the anointing to fall and flow through these men you have appointed. By their hands, let many notable miracles be done. So saturate them that even their shadow is anointed by God to heal. I rebuke every hinderance. Let the Holy Ghost be poured out with purpose!"

Fervent prayer is contagious. In my travels, I've noticed that the powerful apostolic churches in our fellowship have a culture of fervent prayer. It's not just a few; it's a practice of leaders and saints, youth, and elders. At some point in the history of those churches, someone struck the match of fervency, and it caught the whole church on fire!

- Fervent prayer draws the angels of the Lord!
- Fervent prayer moves mountains!
- Fervent prayer drives out the enemy!
- Fervent prayer will break the chains!
- Fervent prayer destroys the yokes!
- Fervent prayer opens doors!
- Fervent prayer breaks down strongholds!

The writer of Hebrews is calling to us:

> Let us therefore come boldly unto the throne of
> grace, that we may obtain mercy, and find grace
> to help in time of need. (Heb. 4:16 KJV)

Element 4: Consistency

One of the most effective and powerfully used apostolic leaders in the history of the entire church age was the apostle Paul.

Paul was a true citizen of Rome, educated by the esteemed Rabbi Gamaliel, the paramount scholar among the all apostles, but he was unapologetically apostolic. Paul had one obsession: Jesus Christ and

His sacrifice for sin. Miracles, signs, and wonders followed his ministry. Countless souls were won and influenced by his sacrificial life.

Paul's suffering and trials are well documented. He endured manifold beatings, tragedies, and betrayals. And yet, in spite of his spectacular successes and epic trials, Paul finished his course; he kept the faith.

How was this possible? Paul's radically apostolic life was built on consistent prayer.

Paul's prayers are recorded over and again throughout the thirteen New Testament books he authored. I believe you will find forty-three prayers in his writings.

Dr. Henry M. Morris in his article, "Paul's Prayer Life," noted,

> The apostle Paul was a great man of prayer. He prayed "without ceasing" for the Roman Christians. To the Corinthian church, he wrote: "I thank my God always on your behalf" (1 Corinthians 1:4). Similarly, to the Ephesians: "|I| cease not to give thanks for you, making mention of you in my prayers" (Ephesians 1:16). The same assurance was written to Philippi: "Always in every prayer of mine for you all making request with joy" (Philippians 1:4). And to the Colossians: "For this cause we also, since the day we heard it, do not cease to pray for you" (Colossians 1:9). "We give thanks to God always for you all, making mention of you in our prayers" (1 Thessalonians 1:2). (Institute of Creation Research, January 27, 2010)

Paul prayed all the time, and he commanded believers to do the same. *Pray without ceasing* (1 Thess. 5:17).

So often we hear about the importance of having a relationship with God. Prayer, conversation with God, is how we maintain and grow our relationship with Him. This statement may seem a little elementary, but you might be surprised how many people claim to know about the importance of prayer but fail to pray consistently.

Over the years, I have learned that consistency in my prayer life is an important key to consistent demonstration of the Spirit in my ministry.

Think about it: the more we pray, the more we understand God and His ways. Our greater measure of understanding allows us to employ more wisdom in the way we operate in our giftings and callings. Operating with wisdom means there are less ministry missteps, which allows us to develop greater confidence in the calling and giftings of God. Confidence produces boldness. Finally, boldness allows us to maximize demonstration of the Spirit: spiritual gifts and fivefold ministry. God is honored, and His work is multiplied. It's all born out of consistent prayer.

This is the reason that consistent prayer is a nonnegotiable in my life. It is the foundation of my life. It is the air I breathe. Without it, I don't have Him. And without Him, I am nothing.

The failure of every fallen apostolic leader was first a failure to pray. You don't want to be a leader with big dreams but a small prayer life. It's a problem if you want to tell people to take up their bed and walk but won't get out of their bed and pray. It's a problem if you want to have the ministry of the apostolic Paul but you don't want to pay the price of consistency.

Do you remember the parable that Jesus gave in Luke 18?

> And he spake a parable unto them to this end, that men ought always to pray, and not to faint; Saying, There was in a city a judge, which feared not God, neither regarded man: And there was a widow in that city; and she came unto him, saying, Avenge me of mine adversary. And he would not for a while: but afterward he said within himself, Though I fear not God, nor regard man; Yet because this widow troubleth me, I will avenge her, lest by her continual coming she weary me. And the Lord said, Hear what the unjust judge

saith. And shall not God avenge his own elect, which cry day and night unto him, though he bear long with them? (Luke 18:1–7 KJV)

When you consistently come before the Lord in consistent radical prayer, our great Judge of the universe is going to respond! Your life and ministry will serve as a welcome mat for God's presence and awesome power!

Element 5: Praying prophetically

You do not need to have the fivefold ministry office of a prophet mentioned in Ephesians 4:11 or the spiritual gift of prophecy listed in 1 Corinthians 12:10 for you to experience and operate in prophetic prayer!

In Ezekiel 37, God commanded Ezekiel to release prophetic prayer over the valley that was full of dry bones.

Not once did God require Ezekiel to conjure up his own word of prophecy. Not once did God expect Ezekiel to operate in his own human wisdom, power, or authority.

Yes, God told Ezekiel to prophesy over His mighty army, but God said,

> Prophesy upon these bones, and *say unto them*, O ye dry bones, hear the word of the Lord. (Ezek. 37:4 KJV)

God gave Ezekiel the powerful prophetic words to say! The resurrection of the mighty army was not a problem left for Ezekiel to solve; the answer was placed in his mouth!

In verse 7, Ezekiel said, "So I prophesied as I was commanded: and as I prophesied [the already powerful and already spoken Word of the Lord], there was a noise, shaking, bones came together."

In verse 10 of that same chapter, after the breath of God came into them, those dry bones stood upon their feet and became an exceeding great army.

When the prophetic "Word of the Lord" was released by God's servant, death was no match, nature was no match, and impossibilities were no match for the ministry of radical prophetic prayer!

Dominion was released; authority was recognized through the operation of a ministry fueled by radical prophetic prayer!

Much like Ezekiel's vision. The enemy is hard at work trying to turn the army of God into a valley dry bones. He wants to silence their voices and turn their dream into dust.

However, God's people must understand that God has placed the prophetic words in our mouths. It's time to release God's resurrection power through prophetic prayer to restore, revive, renew, and resurrect our families, churches, cities, and nations!

We, God's apostolic, end-time army, have countless prophetic words given to us by the Lord Himself. We can declare those prophetic words daily, in every situation, which will release God's authority, dominion, and sovereign power!

God wants me to prophetically declare these words over you, your ministry, your city, and your nations, but the Lord wants you to begin prophetically releasing these words daily as well:

- The fields in your city are white unto harvest—prophesy it!
- These signs shall follow them that believe—prophesy it!
- You, child of God, are blessed indeed and highly favored—prophesy it!
- The gifts of the Spirit are in you and for you—prophesy it!
- The Lord will enlarge your territory—prophesy it!
- Radical submission, radical humility, and radical sacrifice are yours—prophesy it!
- Anointing, power, dominion, and protection are yours—prophesy it!
- There is radically apostolic power in the operation of the ministry of prophetic prayer!
- Prophesy the "Word of the Lord" over your family, ministry, church, city, and nation. Watch the "Word of the Lord" work mightily on your behalf to accomplish His kingdom purpose!

Note: I would like to share a list of prophetic prayers my wife and I pray daily over our family, ministry, and travels:

- I prophesy that the fruit of the spirit is active and evident in our ministry now.
- I prophesy that the gift of a word of wisdom is active in our ministry now.
- I prophesy that the gift of a word of knowledge is active in our ministry now.
- I prophesy that the gift of discerning of spirits is active in our ministry now.
- I prophesy that the gift of faith is active in our ministry now.
- I prophesy that the gifts of healing are active in our ministry now.
- I prophesy that the gift of working miracles is active in our ministry now.
- I prophesy that diverse tongues and interpretation of tongues is active in our ministry now.
- I prophesy that the gift of prophecy is active in our ministry now.
- I prophesy that you will bless us indeed now.
- I prophesy that you will enlarge our territory now.
- I prophesy that we will not cause harm.
- I prophesy that your hand would be with us.
- I prophesy that you would keep us from evil.
- I prophesy to the North, East, South, and West that you will yield global harvest now.
- I prophesy that everywhere we set down our feet we will have mighty harvest, mighty dominion, mighty authority, and mighty healing/miracles.
- I prophesy that our spiritual eyes will be open so we can see that they that be for us are more than they that be against us.
- I prophesy that we will walk by faith and not by sight.

- I prophesy that angels will go before us, walk with us, keep us, and work on our behalf everywhere we go.
- I prophesy that you will bless our finances abundantly.
- I prophesy protection when we travel.
- I prophesy anointing, power, and dominion daily.
- I prophesy divine health over our family.
- I prophesy spiritual growth, depth, exposure, anointing, and ministry over our family.
- I prophesy that every church we walk into there will be a nuclear bomb of faith that strikes the church immediately.

Remember: As you pray prophetically, pray with expectation! Get excited about the word of God you are declaring. Begin to envision those things as already possessed or achieved. See those prophetic statements as fulfilled and not pending.

Note: Below you will find a small portion of the prophetic Word of God that I like to release daily over our family, ministry, God's global work, and our kingdom future:

> And these signs shall follow them that believe; In my name shall they cast out devils; they shall speak with new tongues; They shall take up serpents; and if they drink any deadly thing, it shall not hurt them; they shall lay hands on the sick, and they shall recover. (Mark 16:17–18 KJV)

> Verily, verily, I say unto you, He that believeth on me, the works that I do shall he do also; and greater works than these shall he do; because I go unto my Father. And whatsoever ye shall ask in my name, that will I do, that the Father may be glorified in the Son. If ye shall ask any thing in my name, I will do it. (John 14:12–14 KJV)

> And such as do wickedly against the covenant shall he corrupt by flatteries: but the people

that do know their God shall be strong, and do exploits. (Dan. 11:32 KJV)

The glory of this latter house shall be greater than of the former, saith the Lord of hosts: and in this place will I give peace, saith the Lord of hosts. (Hag. 2:9 KJV)

And it shall come to pass in the last days, saith God, I will pour out of my Spirit upon all flesh: and your sons and your daughters shall prophesy, and your young men shall see visions, and your old men shall dream dreams: And on my servants and on my handmaidens I will pour out in those days of my Spirit; and they shall prophesy. (Acts 2:17–18 KJV)

Say not ye, There are yet four months, and then cometh harvest? behold, I say unto you, Lift up your eyes, and look on the fields; for they are white already to harvest. (John 4:35 KJV)

And Jabez called on the God of Israel, saying, Oh that thou wouldest bless me indeed, and enlarge my coast, and that thine hand might be with me, and that thou wouldest keep me from evil, that it may not grieve me! And God granted him that which he requested. (1 Chron. 4:10 KJV)

When we come into any city or nation in the name of Jesus, the "Word of the Lord" that we prophetically release into the atmosphere will never return void!

So shall my word be that goeth forth out of my mouth: it shall not return unto me void, but it shall accomplish that which I please, and it shall prosper in the thing whereto I sent it. (Isa. 55:11 KJV)

The "Word of the Lord" that we declare will begin to work on our behalf before we even sow the first seeds into the fields!

I sent you to reap that whereon ye bestowed no labour: other men laboured, and ye are entered into their labours. (John 4:38 KJV)

3

RADICAL SUBMISSION

Ability to resist temptation is directly proportionate to your submission to God.

—*Ed Cole*

Submission is the willingness to give up our right to ourselves, to freely surrender our insistence on having our own way all the time.

—*Myles Munroe*

True strength lies in submission which permits one to dedicate his life, through devotion, to something beyond himself.

—*Henry Miller*

Submit yourselves therefore to God. Resist the devil, and he will flee from you. (Jas. 4:7 KJV)

THE GREAT DECEPTION

The enemy has thrown a great net of deception over our world. The deception is this: authority is a bad word; people with authority are bad people. Are you noticing this sentiment? We are living in an anti-authority world!

This is why the apostle Paul said,

> And be not conformed to this world: but be ye transformed by the renewing of your mind, that ye may prove what is that good, and acceptable, and perfect, will of God. (Rom. 12:2 KJV)

It is a shame that this world hates authority, because submission to authority is her cure.

Submission to authority will break the demonic works of lawlessness, hatred, racism, and rebellion.

The Word of God calls us to submit to the leadership that God has placed over us.

> Submit yourselves to every ordinance of man for the Lord's sake: whether it be to the king, as supreme; Or unto governors, as unto them that are sent by him for the punishment of evildoers, and for the praise of them that do well. For so is the will of God, that with well doing ye may put to silence the ignorance of foolish men: As free, and not using your liberty for a cloke of maliciousness, but as the servants of God. Honour all men. Love the brotherhood. Fear God. Honour the king. (1 Pet. 2:13–17 KJV)

> Let every soul be subject unto the higher powers. For there is no power but of God: the powers that be are ordained of God. Whosoever therefore resisteth the power, resisteth the ordinance of God: and they that resist shall receive to themselves damnation. For rulers are not a terror to good works, but to the evil. Wilt thou then not be afraid of the power? do that which is good,

and thou shalt have praise of the same: For he is
the minister of God to thee for good. But if thou
do that which is evil, be afraid; for he beareth not
the sword in vain: for he is the minister of God,
a revenger to execute wrath upon him that doeth
evil. Wherefore ye must needs be subject, not
only for wrath, but also for conscience sake. For
this cause pay ye tribute also: for they are God's
ministers, attending continually upon this very
thing. (Rom. 13:1–6 KJV)

If we want to see a radical demonstration of the Spirit in our
church, ministry, city, or nation, we must throw off the great deception of anti-authority. We must embrace a life of radical submission
to God-ordained authority!

Reverend Michael Robinson, who was partly responsible for
inspiring me to write this book, made this statement, "Submission is
the instant, willing obedience to a lawful order."

Our adversary, the devil, is keen to entice us into anti-authority
attitudes and behaviors, but we will never be a true servant of the
Lord until we practice radical submission. Without it, we will never
be used by God in any significant way. We may teach or preach, but
we will not have signs, wonders, miracles, and following. Our ministries will be void of harvest, radical demonstration, and power.

Submission to spiritual authority also provides a safety net for
our entire household and keeps our children far away from destruction that rebellion brings.

In Matthew 8:8–10, we find a powerful principle of submission. A Roman centurion has approached Jesus to ask if He would
heal his servant. Jesus agrees and offers to go with him to his home.

The centurion answered and said, Lord, I am not
worthy that thou shouldest come under my roof:
but speak the word only, and my servant shall be
healed. For I am a man under authority, having
soldiers under me: and I say to this man, Go, and

he goeth; and to another, Come, and he cometh; and to my servant, Do this, and he doeth it. When Jesus heard it, he marvelled, and said to them that followed, Verily I say unto you, I have not found so great faith, no, not in Israel. (Matt. 8:8–10 KJV)

And Jesus said unto the centurion, Go thy way; and as thou hast believed, so be it done unto thee. And his servant was healed in the selfsame hour. (Matt. 8:13 KJV)

The principle is clear. If we are submitted to authority, we will have greater understanding about how authority works. People who refuse to submit to authority are dangerous to the kingdom of God, because they leverage it the wrong way.

Without submission, there is no possible way for us to appropriately operate in realm of demonstration and power. We will destroy others, not build up, and ultimately destroy ourselves.

THE HISTORY OF REBELLION

The first mention of the anti-authority spirit in human history was instigated by Satan, who was demoted because of his own act of rebellion prior to creation. Satan, in the form of a serpent, engaged Eve in a conversation and openly questioned and contradicted the Word of God:

Now the serpent was more subtil than any beast of the field which the Lord God had made. And he said unto the woman, Yea, hath God said, Ye shall not eat of every tree of the garden? (Gen. 3:1 KJV)

And the serpent said unto the woman, Ye shall not surely die. (Gen. 3:4 KJV)

Satan pressed Eve to question the promises of God, the motives of God, and even the authority of God.

Satan planted a seed of rebellion in the heart of Eve which ultimately led to catastrophe for the human race. God ultimately showed Adam and Eve mercy, but they placed unnecessary pain and misery in their lives and ours as well.

We should be careful that we do not take Satan's bait of rebellion. Like Adam and Eve, we will discover there are many unintended results for anti-authority behavior. We will quickly find ourselves displaced, on the outside looking in, wondering what in the world happened!

Also, by rejecting God-given authority, we will not only hurt ourselves but our families. Adam and Eve must have often looked at their sons sweating in the hot fields and regretfully remembered their rebellion.

SUBMISSION TO WHOM?

There seems to be a trend in the church world. It seems that men and women aspiring to ministry would rather be guided by a committee of peers than by a pastor with real authority. Why is this such a popular practice? True submission is never required of a such a committee. The path to power is not guided by a committee; it's led by true shepherds.

Do you have a pastor? If you desire to be mightily used of God, if you desire to see the ceiling removed from your calling, there is no substitute for having a pastor in your life!

While it is permissible to have mentors who (with your pastor's permission) impart methodology or exposure you to greater apostolic understanding, there must be one spiritual leader: a pastor, who has the final say. You need a pastor in your life whom you will not resist because they have veto power.

There is no place in God's kingdom for those who will not submit to spiritual authority.

Jesus made this declaration about His kingdom:

> Jesus answered, My kingdom is not of this world:
> *if my kingdom were of this world, then would my*
> *servants fight*, that I should not be delivered to the
> Jews: but now is my kingdom not from hence.
> (John 18:36 KJV)

When God's servants refuse to fight earthly anti-authority battles, it's evidence that their kingdom is not of this world. Remember, we are *in* this world but not *of* this world. God's servants are fighting the right battles, not the wrong ones. We don't wrestle flesh and blood; we fight spiritual battles. However, if we are always chest-bumping with earthly authority, fighting flesh and blood, we're essentially telling everyone which world we are *really* from.

When we enter into in the kingdom of God by being born again of the water and the Spirit, we take on a new nature.

It was the apostle Paul who said in 2 Corinthians 5:17 (KJV), "Therefore if any man be in Christ, he is a new creature: old things are passed away; behold, all things are become new."

The anti-authority attitude is a product of our old nature; it's supposed to be discontinued. Submission is the new and improved product of our redeemed nature produced by the power of God.

This new nature allows us to embrace and joyfully obey the admonitions of the Word of God.

> Obey them that have the rule over you, and submit yourselves: for they watch for your souls, as they that must give account, that they may do it with joy, and not with grief: for that is unprofitable for you. (Heb. 13:17 KJV)

Likewise, ye younger, submit yourselves unto the elder. Yea, all of you be subject one to another, and be clothed with humility: for God resisteth the proud, and giveth grace to the humble. Humble yourselves therefore under the mighty hand of God, that he may exalt you in due time. (1 Pet. 5:5–6 KJV)

Let's get real for a moment; we may not enjoy the personality of everyone God places over us. We may not agree with everyone that God places over us. But we will never find a single scripture that encourages us to resist, reject, or rebel against the spiritual authority God placed in our life!

Even when our spiritual authority is wrong. Even when spiritual authority makes a bad judgment call. Even if they offend us with their words, actions, or attitudes. There is no scripture for packing our bags, finding a new pastor, or finding another church! There are a lot of scriptures that would tell us to go to them and be reconciled, to speak truth in love, and to do the hard work of peacemaking.

This being said, the real power to submit comes from being a true spirit-filled citizen of God's great kingdom.

Now unto him that is able to do exceeding abundantly above all that we ask or think, according to the power that worketh in us. (Eph. 3:20 KJV)

SUBMISSION: THE GOOD, BAD, AND UGLY

There are three classic Bible stories related to submission that I classify as good, bad, and ugly. Let's get started!

The good story

In 1 Samuel 24, it tells us a harrowing story about a time when King Saul and three thousand of his went hunting in the rocky hills of Engedi. It was "open season" on David, the son of Jesse. His crime?

He slew a giant and became a national hero. A spirit jealousy had wormed its way into Saul's heart. Israel's king was spiraling into severe paranoia.

David's God-given success caused the positionally minded king to feel threatened and opened his life to demonic deception. Saul had convinced himself that David was chasing the throne, but David was simply submitted to God's voice.

Because David understood the value of submission, he refused to challenge his king's authority even though Saul was totally wrong!

Until this episode, David had such loyalty and love for leadership he would not strike back against a leader that God himself had rejected.

As the story unfolds, Saul finds a cave among the craggy rocks and is completely unaware that the cave he's chosen is where David and his men are hiding!

David's men are convinced that God has delivered their insane oppressor to them on a silver platter! They encourage David to finish the job. But David simply can't bring himself to harm his king. He simply crawls up to sleeping Saul and cuts off a piece of his robe. Sounds like mercy, right? David must feel good about himself, right?

> And it came to pass afterward, that David's heart smote him, because he had cut off Saul's skirt. And he said unto his men, The LORD forbid that I should do this thing unto my master, the LORD's anointed, to stretch forth mine hand against him, seeing he is the anointed of the LORD. So David stayed his servants with these words, and suffered them not to rise against Saul. But Saul rose up out of the cave, and went on his way. (1 Sam. 24:5–7 KJV)

Although David doesn't even touch Saul, the seemingly insignificant act of cutting the robe of his authority breaks his heart. David knows that he has dipped his toes in the pool of rebellion.

It isn't David's job to deal with Saul; it's God's. Conviction grips his heart. Rather than justify his actions, he repents in front of his men.

It was a watershed moment for the young man who would become king of Israel.

Friends, do not resist spiritual authority. Do not rise up against God's appointed leader in your life! Stay in submission, even if being in submission is to the point of being extreme like David. God sees your humility and will exalt you in due time.

The bad story

> And Miriam and Aaron spake against Moses.
> (Num. 12:1 KJV)

The backstory really doesn't matter. These seven words are all that mattered to God! God did not care what their argument involved. God did not care if Miriam and Aaron were right and Moses was wrong.

The brother and sister banded together and pushed back on God's extension of authority in their lives. Notice they didn't raise a hand against Moses; they just opened their mouths.

There is no area where we systematically violate God's standards of submission more than in our ethics of speech. We pick up the phone, sit around restaurant tables, go on our favorite online forums, and commit the same sin as Miriam and Aaron.

When Miriam and Aaron spoke against Moses, their problem was not being called into the office with Moses; they were called to the door of the tabernacle by God Himself!

I would encourage you to read the conversation recorded in Numbers 12:5–11. It's terrifying! The Lord of glory is angry as His voice booms from the cloud. See how God stands up for His man and utterly rebukes those who would open their mouths against him. I would not want to be in Miriam or Aaron's sandals for all the crown jewels in the Tower of London!

And the anger of the LORD was kindled against them; and he departed. And the cloud departed from off the tabernacle; and, behold, Miriam became leprous, white as snow: and Aaron looked upon Miriam, and, behold, she was leprous. (Num. 12:9–10 KJV)

Although God would ultimately spare Miriam at Moses's request, she was put out of the camp for seven days. Three million people had to wait for Miriam's "time-out" to finish.

Let us not convince ourselves that God looks the other way when we disparage our leaders with our words. Their failures may embolden our criticisms, but our dishonoring words may be a greater concern to God than their failure.

The ugly story

Our final story found in Numbers 16 takes rebellion a step further than Miriam and Aaron.

A powerful Hebrew by the name of Korah is dissatisfied with his family's role as carriers of the portable tabernacles and its holy contents. He wants his family to be priests. He feels that Moses and Aaron are hoarding power, that they've gone too far with their authority. However, he does more than speak against their authority; he marshals an uprising of prominent influencers against Moses and Aaron.

And they rose up before Moses, with certain of the children of Israel, two hundred and fifty princes of the assembly, famous in the congregation, men of renown: And they gathered themselves together against Moses and against Aaron, and said unto them, Ye take too much upon you, seeing all the congregation are holy, every one of them, and the LORD is among them: wherefore

then lift ye up yourselves above the congregation
of the LORD? (Num. 16:2–3 KJV)

Moses is grieved by the reckless rally. Moses reminds Korah that his rebellion is not an act against his personal authority but God's. He challenges Korah to a test, calling him and his followers to the sanctuary the next morning to offer incense before the Lord. Moses defers to the Lord to choose among them who is holy.

The next day was a complete catastrophe for Korah and his campaign. The two hundred fifty men who offered incense to the Lord were consumed with fire. Korah, his cohorts, their families, and possessions were swallowed up by the earth. The following day fourteen thousand seven hundred sympathizers perished as well.

Korah was convinced that he had a just cause. But he lost touch with one critical truth: God hates rebellion and those who will join her parade.

Let us be careful. Let us not lose reverence for God and the authority He has placed over us. We must resist the anti-authority spirit of this world! We are wise to submit when we disagree. In fact, disagreement is a revealer of true submission.

There will always be a ministry-altering price to pay when one disregards, dismisses, questions, disrespects, challenges, or rebels against spiritual authority! And whether we like it or not, we will not be the only person who pays the price for our rebellion. Like Korah, our families will pay the price as well.

The good news is, God allows us time and space to repent so we can know the value of spiritual submission to authority.

If we confess our sins, he is faithful and just to
forgive us our sins, and to cleanse us from all
unrighteousness. (1 John 1:9 KJV)

LIFT THEIR HANDS

We can do so much more than simply submit to our leaders; we can fully support the leaders God has graciously placed in our lives.

Let's look at one more story in the life of the great leader, Moses.

During the Israelites' time in the wilderness, the Amalekites came up against them in battle. Moses had given word to Joshua to lead men out to fight the Amalekites. He assured Joshua that he would stand on top of the hill with the staff of God raised.

As battle ensued, Moses noticed that as long as he held up his arms, the Israelites prevailed, but whenever he lowered his arms, the Amalekites prevailed. Obviously, Moses held his arms high, but soon, as you can well imagine, his arms became tired. Aaron and Hur, seeing Moses's dilemma, took a stone and placed under Moses so he could be seated, and they each held up one of Moses's arms, and Israel prevailed (Exod. 17:8–16).

The small support that Hur and Aaron provided Moses on that day had an incredible outcome.

This story perfectly illustrates that people in authority can become weary and need people to support their important work. It should be the goal of every apostolic to not only submit but take a little load off those who lead us. This support, small as it may seem, could be one of the greatest investments of our lives.

When you read about authority in scripture, you will quickly find the principle of honor.

> Let the elders that rule well be counted worthy of double honour, especially they who labour in the word and doctrine. (1 Tim. 5:17 KJV)

> Honour all men. Love the brotherhood. Fear God. Honour the king. (1 Pet. 2:17 KJV)

> Honor thy father and mother. (Eph. 6:2 KJV)

The word *honor* means to esteem, to value, to *show* great respect. Here is my point: submission is not just an attitude; it's action.

We show submission through words!

- We show submission through our attitudes!

- We show submission through our obedience!
- We show submission through trust!
- We show submission through love!
- We show submission by not challenging leadership!
- We show submission by not questioning authority!
- We show submission by collaborating, cooperating, and communicating with our leaders!

Let's not forget to demonstrate submission by praying for our spiritual authority. We can break the back of the spirit of rebellion by serving as a prayer covering for those who lead us.

The leaders of the New Testament coveted prayer.

> Brethren, pray for us. (1 Thess. 5:25 KJV)

> Finally, brethren, pray for us, that the word of the Lord may have free course, and be glorified, even as it is with you. (2 Thess. 3:1 KJV)

> Pray for us: for we trust we have a good conscience, in all things willing to live honestly. (Heb. 13:18 KJV)

Something dynamic begins to happen when we pray for our pastor! Something powerful happens when we become the lifter of the arms of our spiritual leader! Praying for our leaders will cause us to love and not question authority! Those prayers will cause us to want to submit to authority. Those prayers will cause us to reject and resist the anti-authority spirit of this world.

EXAMPLES OF RADICAL SUBMISSION

If you want an unobstructed view of radical submission, watch the drama that unfolded in Genesis 16. Abram has a promise from God that he would be a father. His wife Sarai is barren. Sarai convinces Abram to take her servant Hagar as his second wife so he can have a child. So Abram starts hanging out with Hagar, and she conceives. When Hagar conceives, Sarai becomes insanely jealous and tells Abram that Hagar is disrespecting her. The claws are out. Abram is in the middle. We pick up the conversation from there:

> But Abram said unto Sarai, Behold, thy maid is in thy hand; do to her as it pleaseth thee. And when Sarai dealt hardly with her, she fled from her face. And the angel of the Lord found her by a fountain of water in the wilderness, by the fountain in the way to Shur. And he said, Hagar, Sarai's maid, whence camest thou? and whither wilt thou go? And she said, I flee from the face of my mistress Sarai. And the angel of the Lord said unto her, Return to thy mistress, and submit thyself under her hands. And the angel of the Lord said unto her, I will multiply thy seed exceedingly, that it shall not be numbered for multitude. (Gen. 16:6–10 KJV)

Wow! Hagar, go back and submit. Yes, she's crazy jealous, but she is your authority. If you will do that, I will bless you!

Let's be honest. Submission is not as complicated as we like to make it out to be! We often get very creative weaving a beautiful tapestry of justification as to why we "fired" our authority and found someone with better people skills. Be careful! It's not worth it; you might have an easier life for a while, but you will forfeit God's power and blessings.

I first began to get clarity about the value, power, and beauty of radical submission to apostolic authority during the Ethiopia crusade in March 2000.

During one of those truly radically apostolic prayer meetings, one of the leaders, a veteran apostolic leader in our movement, feeling led of the Holy Ghost, shouted out, "Thus saith the Lord."

Immediately, Bro. Billy Cole said, "Wait!"

That veteran man of God radically submitted, and the gathering of leaders launched back into deep prayer.

A while later, that same veteran apostolic leader, being led of the Spirit, shouted out, "Thus saith the Lord."

Immediately, Bro. Billy Cole stopped him and said, "Wait!"

The veteran apostolic leader submitted himself without hesitation, and we all went right back into the deep places of the Spirit of the Lord with great intensity.

A third time that veteran apostolic leader tried to speak what the Spirit of the Lord was compelling him to speak, and again Bro. Billy Cole stopped him a bit more forcefully.

I felt embarrassed for that man of God. Still, the veteran leader demonstrated no signs of agitation or frustration, just love, respect, and submission to that mighty man of God, Bro. Billy Cole.

A few moments later, Bro. Billy Cole said, "Brother, now is the time. What has the Lord told you to tell us?"

That veteran apostolic leader did not flinch, did not show an ounce of arrogance, nor did he react in any way unseemly; he just boldly and obediently declared the Word of God in the direction of our spiritual leader, Bro. Billy Cole.

The apostle Paul told the young preacher Timothy,

> Thou therefore endure hardness, as a good soldier of Jesus Christ. (2 Tim. 2:3 KJV)

Paul's wise counsel to his young friend is something we should all take into account, especially in the area of submission.

I witnessed another instance of radical submission that involved a different veteran apostolic minister.

Bro. Billy Cole was always very adamant about not preaching lengthy sermons during the crusade services. He gave everyone a specific amount of time in the pulpit, and he expected everyone to submit no matter how they thought or felt in the moment.

One of our team members was preaching powerfully during a morning crusade session. At one point, that veteran minister had all the translators holding him across their arms while he preached the Word of God with passion and authority.

The hundreds of thousands of Ethiopians who were in attendance loved it! They were shouting with him as he preached! It was exciting! The Word was resonating with all of the Ethiopians present.

At some point, the preacher went over his allotted time for preaching. He turned to Bro. Billy Cole in front of the crowd and asked for more time. Bro. Billy Cole did not say a word. He sat there, motionless.

The preacher continued to preach. I am not really sure how long he preached past his allowed time, but to Bro. Billy Cole, one second over the allowed time was rebellion.

The service was great, the people responded, and then we all retired to the bus so we could return to the hotel.

At some point on that long bus ride, Bro. Billy Cole openly rebuked the man in front of the team.

Although I thought a fight would surely break out, God was teaching me a valuable lesson about submission through the rebuke and response of two mighty men of God.

I watched as that veteran apostolic leader submitted himself to Bro. Billy Cole and received public rebuke with joy and gladness.

To see those mighty heroes of the faith, in both accounts, demonstrate radical submission and their positive attitude toward correction was one of the greatest gifts God has ever given to me!

The examples of those two godly men prepared me to correctly respond to the spiritual authority in my own life.

While on active duty military service in the USAF, I served in the 568th Security Police Force on a special unit referred to as Wolfpack. Wolfpack had the privilege of serving as the augmentation security detail for President Clinton on two occasions during his visits to Germany.

During the presidential visits, our team had daily interactions with the Secret Service detail. They would constantly encourage our team to consider applying for a career in the Secret Service following active duty.

When I left active duty military service, we returned to Ypsilanti, MI, and began the application process for employment with the Secret Service. I planned to start as a uniformed agent for the Secret Service and dreamed of one day being able to serve and protect the president of the United States.

The day before leaving for Washington, my pastor, Rev. William Nix, requested breakfast with my wife and me. He had hardly spoken a word to us during the sixty days we spent in Ypsilanti since we returned from active duty. We met at an old restaurant called the Bomber, which was located in a historic part of our city called Depot Town. After ordering our food, he said, "What is your plan?"

I was so excited! I said, "We are going to Washington to take a job as uniformed Secret Service, and we are leaving tomorrow!"

He looked at me and cleared his throat in that terrifying way that only Pastor William Nix could and said, "No, you are not. You are my new youth pastor. Be at the office tomorrow morning at seven a.m."

He stood up, left money on the table, and left the restaurant. There was no discussion. He just shattered our plans and dreams without any compassion, discussion, or compromise.

I looked at my wife, she looked at me, and we never thought one second about rebelling against the man of God. We left the Bomber Restaurant having been bombed, but we rejoiced knowing our pastor was not a man who would tickle our ears while we made the mistake of pursuing our plans. Pastor Nix was directing us down the path that God had for us. It was a greater path than any path we could create for ourselves.

I do not know where we would be today if we had walked out of that restaurant, went home, packed our bags, and flew to Washington against the mandate of our spiritual leader. I can tell you this: it would not have been good. I was twenty-three years old, and my wife was twenty-two, when our great pastor unapologetically crushed our dreams so we could pursue God's dreams.

Don't make the mistake of thinking the decision to submit to our pastor was not easy. It wasn't! As that old song says, "When I look back over my life, and I think things over, I can truly say that I am blessed! I have a testimony!" No, I have thousands of testimonies because I did not allow the enemy to infect me with an anti-authority attitude! We chose God's way of radical submission.

Oh, the path that our pastor wisely placed us on! What a great impact that one brief conversation has had on our lives and many others:

- We have seen hundreds of thousands of people repent of their sins, be filled with the Holy Ghost, and baptized in Jesus's name!
- We have served as UPCI missionaries to Belgium, Switzerland, Austria, Liechtenstein, and Germany.
- We have carried the gospel to approximately one hundred nations in the world.
- We have ministered the gospel in every state in the USA and much of Canada.
- We have witnessed the blind seeing, the deaf hearing, the lame walking, and healing for all manner of disease.
- We have confronted and cast out devils all over the world.
- We are blessed with apostolic friends who are just as radical as we are and are worth more than anything the world could ever give us.
- We have two beautiful daughters who love the Lord and joyfully serve with us.

The world did not give any of those great blessings to us. They are the fruits and rewards of radical submission.

Many radically apostolic men and woman of God can share stories when they under authority that seemed to oppose progress in their ministry. Still, the angel of Lord spoke to them just like the angel of the Lord spoke to Hagar, "If you submit yourself under Sarai's hand, you will be blessed."

We had the privilege of serving Rev. Stephen Merritt as his supervising missionary family during his first AIM trip to the nation of Austria. There are not enough eloquent words to express how proud we are of him and his wife, Angelica. We are beyond thrilled that God has allowed us to serve alongside them both in missions and on crusades.

As we close out this chapter, I would like to include a testimony from Bro. Merritt that powerfully articulates the blessing of radical submission.

*****

It was the year 2010. I was in Winchester, VA, praying in one of our classrooms in my home church when I felt the Lord direct me to investigate the German-Speaking Nations as a possible field of labor.

At this point in my calling, I had not yet heard of Charles Robinette or the revival they had been experiencing through Austria and beyond. The only thing I knew was that God was leading me to this part of the world.

I felt the call of God to pursue the life of a missionary at the young age of nineteen. Five years had passed since that initial call, but that undeniable call to foreign soil remained.

I arrived in Vienna, Austria, in 2011. To say it was a whirlwind of apostolic power and experience is an understatement. God was at work in this nation!

It was in the middle of this great apostolic revival that I arrived at the radical submission milestone. (Talking about it now is easy, but at the moment, it was one of the hardest, terrifying, and crushing trials ever endured.)

Bro. Robinette was away visiting other churches within the region. I was required to make sure the Apostolic Ministry Training Center (AMTC) was operational and running smoothly in Bro. Robinette's absence. I can't say what it was exactly that caused me to undermine this responsibility, but I did. (Even now, reliving this moment brings me to tears.) Word got to Bro. Robinette that school did not start on time and the AMTC module of excellence and apostolic responsibility was broken through my lack of urgency and readiness.

Later that day I received a text from Bro. Robinette expressing his disappointment in my performance and promptness. As I read his message, defiance, self-justification, and self-preservation rose within me. I quickly typed a response. As I typed each letter and word into the message box, my inner glorified conscience was telling me to step back and reconsider. In a fit of defiance, I sent the message.

It was a few days later that I received a reply from Bro. Robinette simply saying, "We'll talk when I get back."

From that moment until the moment he arrived, which was over the course of a weekend, my mind raced, my spirit burned, and my emotions churned within me.

I knew deep down that what I had done was wrong. It was an act of rebellion and defiance. And for the next few days, I lost my appetite to eat, I could not sleep, and my mornings and nights were plagued with great conviction. I felt as though something was building within me that was going to burst forth from the inside out.

Monday finally arrived. Bro. Robinette texted me, asking if I could meet him at his house.

As I sat on the train heading to his house, thoughts raced through my mind: thoughts of what I had done, thoughts of what he was going to say, and thoughts of worst-case scenarios and best-case scenarios.

Powerful emotions were through me. My body literally ached with conviction. As I disembarked the train and boarded the bus, my heart began to race even faster, and my palms began to sweat; something was happening within me that I could not explain. This was not the typical "going to the principal's office" feeling. It was something much more, much more powerful, much more supernatural!

When I finally arrived at Bro. Robinette's house, I stepped down off the bus and began walking toward the front door. I still did not know what I was going to say; as a matter of fact, I had no idea how I was even going to respond. I had to decide to either entertain, follow the spirit of rebellion, and go the way of self-justification and self-preservation or surrender to the evident work of the Holy Ghost.

It was at that moment when I knocked on the front door and Bro. Robinette opened the door. Seeing him standing caused all those emotions and feelings to burst forth into storm of sorrow and repentance. It was supernatural. I physically fell down in the doorway and wrapped my arms around his legs crying out in repentance and submission.

I can look back now at that moment and clearly see without a doubt that it was in that moment of radical submission to God and to the man of God that God allowed something to shift within me that became the catalyst for exponential revival everywhere my feet were planted.

It has now been almost eight years since that milestone. I have seen the mighty hand of God at work in the lives of so many people, from Austria to North America, to the continent of Africa, to the many nations of the South Pacific, and even right here on the tiny island of Samoa. There are *no* substitutes, no replacements, and no alternatives for radical submission."

Rev. Stephen M. Merritt
Missionary to Samoa

*****

When we serve spiritual authority, radically submit to spiritual authority, pray for spiritual authority, trust spiritual authority, honor spiritual authority, and humble ourselves before spiritual authority, God will bless us abundantly!

4

RADICAL HUMILITY

There is nothing noble in being superior to your fellow man; true nobility is being superior to your former self.

—Ernest Hemingway

These are the few ways we can practice humility: To speak as little as possible of one's self. To mind one's own business. Not to want to manage other people's affairs. To avoid curiosity. To accept contradictions and correction cheerfully. To pass over the mistakes of others. To accept insults and injuries. To accept being slighted, forgotten and disliked. To be kind and gentle even under provocation. Never to stand on one's dignity. To choose always the hardest.

—Mother Teresa

If anyone tells you that a certain person speaks ill of you, do not make excuses about what is said of you but answer, "He was ignorant of my other faults, else he would not have mentioned these alone."

—Epictetus

By humility and the fear of the Lord are riches, and honour, and life. (Prov. 22:4 KJV)

And whosoever shall exalt himself shall be abased; and he that shall humble himself shall be exalted. (Matt. 23:12 KJV)

Humility is knowing who you are, knowing who God is, and never getting confused about who is who. One man said, "Humility is not thinking less of yourself, it's thinking of yourself less."

In his great sermon on the mountain, Jesus described humility as being poor in spirit, which means we know how wretched we are without Him.

According to the *Merriam-Webster Dictionary*, humility is defined as "freedom from pride or arrogance."

What a great definition! Humility is freedom from pride. If humility frees us, then we can conclude that pride enslaves us. Only when we've untethered ourselves from pride will we experience true humility.

In ministry, we must remember that pride is an unholy sense of self. Our personal glory is more important than God's glory.

Pride is something we will all battle; it attacks us differently, in different areas of life. Some people battle pride in the area of possessions and wealth. I've known people who had an unhealthy sense of pride in their independent, self-made lifestyle. People's pride can revolve around their education, knowledge, or experience. Talent and giftings are also a common source of pride. Let's also not forget that spiritual pride is a trap that we can fall into also.

Without humility, we will never reach the radical level of apostolic ministry. Consider the following scriptural statements regarding humility:

- Humility is necessary for service in the kingdom of God (Mic. 6:8).
- We are to "put on" humility (Col. 3:12).
- We are to walk with humility (Eph. 4:1–2).
- We are to avoid false humility (Col. 2:18).

- We are to be clothed with humility (1 Pet. 5:5).
- The cry of the humble is heard of God (Ps. 9:12).
- God dwells with and revives the humble (Isa. 57:15).
- The humble that will be delivered by God (Job 22:29).
- The humble will be lifted up by the Lord (Jas. 4:10).
- The humble will be exalted by God (Luke 14:11).
- The humble will be the greatest in God's kingdom (Matt. 18:4).

Although some people reek of pride, it's not always obvious in a life. Some people carefully camouflage their pride knowing that their false humility will garner them more respect.

Solomon wisely observed in Proverbs 16:18 that pride goes before destruction. I have seen the tragedy of a destroyed ministry due to sin. There were some failures that I saw coming from miles away; others came as a complete surprise to me. Their pride and self-will never registered with me.

Pride is one of the most dangerous tools in the enemy's ministry dismantling kit because its presence is often unknown to the host. Pride may cause a person with the least amount of humility to be convinced they have the most. Pride can actually be an unholy motivation that drives a person to excel in kingdom work.

I will never forget a phone conversation I had with a man while planning a crusade which involved several ministers across our fellowship. The man called to tell me that he felt directed to participate in the crusade. I expressed that I was delighted to have him on the team.

The man excitedly shared with me about how God used him in spiritual gifts, how he felt that he would usher the crusade team to dimensions never seen before, and that the world needed to be exposed to his ministry.

The man was completely unaware that his statements were dripping with the spirit of pride. It became clear that the man's vision for the crusade was for himself and his giftings to be exalted. I began to feel grieved in my spirit. I was thinking, *This crusade is about Jesus, not you!*

The more he talked, the more I realized the harm that could be done by allowing that spirit into our efforts. After a few more difficult moments in conversation, I had to excuse him from the crusade.

Over the course of our lives, God will put a few tests in our path to authenticate our humility or to reveal pride.

THREE TESTS OF HUMILITY

Although humility is manifested in a multitude of ways, I feel directed by the Holy Ghost to share three areas that relate to ministry.

1. How we handle promotions in our lives and in the lives of others
2. How we respond to correction and demotions in our lives and in the lives of others
3. How we respond to gossip, slander, and criticism directed at ourselves or our family

Test 1: Promotions of ourselves and others

Promotion in our lives
Do you remember the story of Joseph? He was betrayed by his brothers, torn from his family, sold into slavery, lied about, and forgotten in a nasty Egyptian prison for many years. But in one day, Joseph went from the prison to the palace. Joseph was the most powerful man in Egypt excluding only the pharaoh.

Joseph handled his promotion graciously. He could have easily succumbed to a first-class ego trip. He could have used his newly acquired power to even the score with his brothers.

Joseph's summary of the situation was that God was responsible for the incredible turn of events in his life.

> So now it was not you that sent me hither, but
> God: and he hath made me a father to Pharaoh,
> and lord of all his house, and a ruler throughout
> all the land of Egypt. (Gen. 45:8 KJV)

Whenever we are promoted, elected, or selected, we need to remember that God was responsible. We should also remember that roles and offices are not something we should take ownership of; we are simply stewards of such things.

Success is just as dangerous as failure—sometimes more so. The enemy will work hard to draw us into prideful thinking and attitudes of entitlement or ownership.

On June 3, 2017, Alex Honnold climbed Yosemite Park's three-thousand-foot El Capitan without ropes or a safety harness. It took him three hours and fifty-seven minutes. There was absolutely no room for even one error on the climb. Was he brave or reckless? Your response to that question could be an indicator of your attitude toward safety and risk-taking.

In rock climbing, the higher you climb, the more important safety measures become.

This principle holds true in ministry. The more you are promoted or elevated, the more important it is that you have safety ropes in your life for your protection to keep you on the wall of ministry.

There are four ropes that are important at high altitudes:

- God: Our Lord will always keep our lives pure and humble; He is the one who truly elevates us.
- Pastor: A shepherd will check our motives and make sure we have a strong grip on truth.
- Our spouse: We are unwise to ignore the wisdom and counsel of our spouse; your spouse knows you better than anyone else.
- Friends: We need friends who are not insecure about our promotions and love us enough to tell us if there is error in our life.

We must secure our ministry and family to the ropes that will hold us when the winds pick up on the wall or when our feet begin to slip from fatigue or a misstep.

I have known many truly humble leaders in my life. Men and women who were mightily used by God and yet humble and unassuming. It is clear to see that God raised them up because they were willing to be harnessed to the ropes of authority and healthy relationships. Their ascent in ministry did not change their humility or dependency on God.

Seeing others promoted

Our humility will be tested when we see others promoted, especially when they are promoted to things we had hoped to do.

A story is told of a tourist who watched an old New English fisherman stepping off his boat and lay a bucket full of blue crabs on the pier. The tourist asked, "Why don't you have a lid on that bucket? Aren't you afraid those crabs will escape?"

The fisherman replied, "No need for a lid. Whenever a crab gets to the top of the bucket, the others always pull it down."

Sadly, this is the attitude of our world. *If it's not me, it won't be anyone!* More than a few good men and woman have had the unfortunate experience of people "grabbing their ankles" because God was elevating their ministry.

It may be hard to see someone assume a role that you hoped for. Gifted people can sometimes stir up feelings of self-doubt and insecurity within us. Humility allows us to push past that carnal thinking and celebrate their promotions and kingdom wins.

Be very careful when someone speaks disparagingly about a leader or gifted person. The person may be like one of those crabs just trying to pull that leader down to their level.

King Saul's son, Jonathan, is a great example of how we should react when God elevates another man. In a monarchy, the eldest son is heir; there are no elections.

As a youth, I would imagine that many people talked to, challenged, and encouraged Jonathan regarding his future kingship. No doubt Jonathan, as a boy, thought about the perks of being king. As a young leader, he probably reflected on how he would address the problems and opportunities of Israel during his tenure.

Then, almost out of nowhere, a lad captured the heart of Israel. He defeated the Philistines' greatest warrior in a one-on-one fight to the death. He had talent that would make an insecure man sick. He was as skilled with a harp as a sling. He became the nation's favorite general and musician.

The maidens of Israel would sing, "Saul has slain, his thousands, but David, his ten thousands."

Jonathan was all but pushed out of the picture. It was obvious that God's favor and anointing was flowing away from Jonathan to David. How would you feel about all this if you were in Jonathan's shoes?

Jonathan didn't become bitter or buck God's plan. He refused to treat David as competition. He saw David as a confidant and friend.

> And it came to pass, when he had made an end of speaking unto Saul, that the soul of Jonathan was knit with the soul of David, and Jonathan loved him as his own soul. (1 Sam. 18:1 KJV)

When David was running for his life, Jonathan resourced David and fought to preserve his life.

> And Jonathan stripped himself of the robe that was upon him, and gave it to David, and his garments, even to his sword, and to his bow, and to his girdle. (1 Sam. 18:4 KJV)

If you serve in ministry, sometimes you will dream dreams, and you will see others get there first. God watches our heart and our reactions when we see others promoted. If we can't celebrate and resource others when they are enjoying the favor of the Lord, we can't be trusted with promotion.

Self-promotion

There is no room for arrogance, self-promotion, or pride in the kingdom of our great God. The apostle Paul said it like this:

Let nothing be done through strife or vainglory; but in lowliness of mind let each esteem other better than themselves. Look not every man on his own things, but every man also on the things of others. Let this mind be in you, which was also in Christ Jesus: Who, being in the form of God, thought it not robbery to be equal with God: But made himself of no reputation, and took upon him the form of a servant, and was made in the likeness of men: And being found in fashion as a man, he humbled himself, and became obedient unto death, even the death of the cross. (Phil. 2:3–8 KJV)

A young evangelist called me a few years back and said, "Brother Robinette, I'm constantly under attack. People are always calling me arrogant, prideful, and are talking about me on social media."

He was weeping as he spoke to me about the pain he was enduring due to the gossip, slander, and criticism he was experiencing from his brothers and sisters in Christ. He was so close to quitting the ministry.

While on the call, the Holy Ghost prompted me, and I said, "Brother, let's go to your social media platforms, and let's read your post together and see if we can find any problems."

When we arrived at his Twitter account, I said, "Let me read these tweets to you, and you tell me what you hear." It turned out that his posts were mainly self-focused and self-congratulatory. There was way too much emphasis on self when he shared revival results and not enough glory was being given to God.

I encouraged the young evangelist to delete all the posts and to start a new pattern of honoring God and everyone but himself in everything he posted.

The usage of personal pronouns such as *I* and *me* when declaring the great victories of our Lord is inappropriate in God's kingdom.

True humility will always deflect glory away from ourselves back to God.

Let us not forget those sage words of the apostle Paul:

> I am crucified with Christ: nevertheless I live; *yet not I, but Christ liveth in me*: and the life which I now live in the flesh I live by the faith of the Son of God, who loved me, and gave himself for me. (Gal. 2:20 KJV)

We tell the crusade team members all the time, "When you post about what God has done on this crusade, you honor God, you honor the missionary team on this field, you honor the national church, and you honor your fellow crusade team members, but if you ever honor yourself, you will be on the first flight home."

On January 22, 2014, I preached "Desperate for the Demonstration of the Spirit" at the Because of the Times (BOTT) conference in Alexandria, LA. I was so nervous about preaching at BOTT. I will never forget gathering with all those mighty men and women of God in the office of Pastor Anthony Mangun before the evening service. Pastor Mangun was, of course, sowing faith in our hearts and in the hearts of his team. He was preparing everyone with great excellence for the direction and flow of that BOTT evening service.

Bro. Mangun came over to me in the midst of the meeting and said, "Don't be nervous. This meeting is so important to God, His kingdom, and His people that everyone who preaches is anointed."

That really took the pressure off. I am laughing as I write these words because as sincerely as I could, I said, "Thank you for that word of encouragement, Bro. Mangun."

But inside I was thinking, *Great, no pressure now!*

While I add that part humorously, there was no doubt that God gave me a word for His people and a special anointing for His kingdom moment.

As I was leaving Bro. Mangun's office that night, the Lord spoke to me and said, "This is not your moment. This is my moment. You could speak the word of faith for miracles tonight because those gifts operate in you, but you would teach my people so much more if you would be willing to decrease so that others could increase."

The Lord directed me to invite Missionary Nathan Harrod to the platform and have him speak the word of faith for miracles, signs, and wonders for God's people.

I was so nervous to ask Bro. Mangun for permission. I pulled him aside and said, "Sir, God told me to use Bro. Nathan Harrod at the end of the message tonight to pray the prayer of faith."

Bro. Mangun looked at me and said, "Bro. Robinette, do whatever God told you to do! Just do it within your time slot."

That night, when Bro. Nathan Harrod spoke the word of faith, the Lord moved in a mighty way with impartation of apostolic gifting; there were many notable miracles, and God was glorified!

On September 27, 2017, I preached a sermon at the UPCI General Conference, Global Missions service, entitled, "This is the Greatest Hour of the Church."

The Lord spoke to me and said, "My people need apostolic exposure and impartation." Then the Lord directed me to incorporate as many apostolic voices as time would permit into the message He would deliver during that service. The Lord told me to use Bro. James Corbin, Bro. Nathan Hulsman, Bro. Michael Ensey, Bro. Art Wilson, Bro. David Bounds, Bro. Jimmy Stark, Bishop Jim Stark, Bishop Mark Morgan, and Bro. Eli Hernandez to impart faith for unprecedented demonstration, power, and sacrifice unto His people.

Following the service, a minister came up to me on the side of the platform and said, "Bro. Robinette, that was your moment. You may never get it again. Why would you share your moment in front of the UPCI ministerial constituency with other people?"

I was dumbfounded by the question, and I said, "No, sir, that was not my moment. That was God's moment, and God had a plan for His kingdom that did not involve me getting the glory or seeking the praises of men."

We should never view the gifts and opportunities God has graciously given us as exclusively ours. We should always listen to the voice of God and seek to involve and bless others.

Self-promotion is the fruit of an independent spirit. There's no room for anyone else. Some people try to sanctify their independent spirit by convincing themselves that they are too spiritual to be understood and everyone else is too carnal. Independence is overrated. We need a revival of apostolic codependency. We need God and each other.

Yes, there have been times when God used only one man or woman, but He prefers to work through unity and community.

Ecclesiastes 4:9–12 tells us that two are better than one, and a threefold cord is not quickly broken.

Jesus set a powerful precedent for the apostles in Mark 6 by sending them out two by two. In Luke 10, he repeats this example.

In the book of Acts, the church's codependency produces demonstration and power that explodes off the pages of scripture.

The apostle Paul highlighted the codependency of the church in 1 Corinthians 12:

> But now are they many members, yet but one body. And the eye cannot say unto the hand, I have no need of thee: nor again the head to the feet, I have no need of you. Nay, much more those members of the body, which seem to be more feeble, are necessary: And those members of the body, which we think to be less honourable, upon these we bestow more abundant honour; and our uncomely parts have more abundant comeliness. For our comely parts have no need: but God hath tempered the body together, having given more abundant honour to that part which lacked: That there should be no schism in the body; but that the members should have the same care one for another. (1 Cor. 12:20–25 KJV)

Ephesians 4:11–12 reveals that the fivefold ministry of apostles, prophets, evangelists, pastors, and teachers work together equipping God's people for the work of ministry.

Promote others

We are responsible for the apostolic development of the ministries and giftings of our brothers and sisters. We are custodians of the call of God upon the lives of God's people under our authority.

We have served and led crusades teams all over the world, but we learned a valuable lesson from Bishop Daniel Garlitz, who served as the Malawi A-Team leader for about a decade.

I cannot remember a time that Bishop Garlitz ever put himself on the crusade team preaching or teaching schedule. Many times, we would try to encourage him to minister in our place, but he would always shut down our attempts to honor him with a soft but terrifying, "Now, brethren." Those two words brought a conclusion to many of our discussions.

Bishop Garlitz would always tell us, "The Lord wants me to facilitate your ministries."

Bishop Garlitz was so passionate about the development of our apostolic ministries. He was so committed to ensuring our spiritual maturity and providing opportunities for us to grow in the gifts of the Spirit.

Bishop Garlitz made the team depend on each other's gifting and ministries, and he resisted every impression of selfishness or self-promotion. He was a builder of apostolic men and an instructor of apostolic methodology.

When we began to lead our own teams, we realized that every good thing we ever experienced during the Malawi A-Team crusades resulted from the radical humility, unity, and mutual apostolic dependency that Bishop Garlitz fostered in us during our travels.

As we prepared team-ministry schedules in the crusades we were leading, I refused to put myself on the schedule. Yes, I can speak the word of faith. Yes, I am anointed and gifted to release God's Word and power into the crowds of many thousands of people, but kingdom moments belong to God.

Prior to the crusades we coordinate, we incorporate three days of crusade team training which includes apostolic instruction and apostolic impartation.

The Lord has given us a vision and a plan for global apostolic training and global apostolic impartation that would facilitate millions of His people being exposed to, trained in, and released like a tsunami to capture God's global harvest.

Because God's kingdom and blessings are not about us, we should

- give it away,
- share it,
- involve as many as you can,
- promote everyone you can,
- provide apostolic exposure to everyone you can,
- create apostolic training opportunities for everyone you can, and
- hold nothing back!

As long as we keep an open hand in ministry, God will keep filling everything back up, pressed down, shaken together, and running over! Hallelujah!

God can do so much more through us when we operate as a team and facilitate and celebrate each other's calling, gifting, and ministry.

Test 2: Correction and demotion

At the funeral service for Rev. Billy Cole, Bishop Jim Stark requested for all the Ethiopia crusade team members to stand, and then he made the statement, "We have all been through the Billy Cole School of Ministry, and we all have the scars to prove it."

Everyone in the building laughed, but some of us winced from the memory of painful but oh so critical, apostolic correction and instruction that Rev. Billy Cole heaped lovingly upon those who would receive.

If you resist the correction of someone who loves you, you are not humble. If you do not come to love and appreciate those moments of correction, you are not humble.

In 1999, when we first began to operate in the gifts of the Spirit, we saw multitudes filled with the Holy Ghost and baptized in Jesus's name as we traveled and evangelized around the United States and Canada.

During this new season, I received a phone call from a pastor who wanted me to come to his church to minister. He told me on the phone that their church would have at least one hundred people that needed the Holy Ghost when we arrived. I'm not sure whether the pastor's statement was wishful thinking or misrepresentation, but when I arrived, there were less than ten people in the church and only one person who needed the Holy Ghost.

During the whole service, I sat there on that small platform of that little church feeling angry! I felt like I had been misled and disrespected. Surely, this was poor stewardship of my time and giftings. (Yes, I was wrong!)

When they very kindly introduced me, I took the pulpit and angrily spoke these words, "I'm not preaching for just one soul! Bring that man to the front and I'll pray him through to the Holy Ghost."

The man came to the front; he was immediately filled with the Holy Ghost with the evidence of speaking with other tongues. The fact of his new birth into God's kingdom was not a validation of my carnal behavior. It was the mercy of God upon that man's soul. It was also the mercy of God that I wasn't struck down in the pulpit by the wrath of God.

As I walked out the door of that sanctuary that evening, my cell phone began to ring. It was Rev. Billy Cole, and he was not happy! When I said hello, I was certain I would have an ally when I told him what that church had done to me. But Rev. Billy Cole's first words out of his mouth were, "You stupid, arrogant boy! What have you done?"

He told me that while he was praying, the Lord revealed to him the sin of my pride and arrogance. He said, "Get on an airplane and fly to West Virginia and come to my house. Cancel your preaching schedule. If you survive me, you might preach again!"

When the man of God spoke, it was as if someone flipped on a light switch. I could instantly see how prideful I had been. I was wrong. My heart was broken. I was the man of sin.

The words of the prophet Nathan to King David came like thunder into my spiritual system.

> And Nathan said to David, Thou art the man…
> Wherefore hast thou despised the command-
> ment of the LORD, to do evil in his sight? (2 Sam.
> 12:7, 9 KJV)

Immediately, with tears streaming down my face, I began to make calls and cancel services. I purchased an airplane ticket to West Virginia to meet with Rev. Billy Cole. It would not be one of the more enjoyable times at Bro. Cole's home, but it would prove to be most profitable to my life.

Over three days, Bro. Cole spiritually shredded me. He spiritually stripped me of arrogance and pride. I do not remember everything he said, but it was both painful and humbling, that is for sure.

At some point, he said, "Get up off the floor. Stop repenting. No more tears. You are ready to be used by God again."

He prayed for me and with me. He imparted apostolic seed back into my hands and sent me back into God's harvest field.

Handling personal demotions and the demotion of others
Prior to becoming fully appointed missionaries, Stacey and I spent time overseas assisting veteran missionaries.

In one endeavor, we assisted a missionary by overseeing his work while he and his family returned to the States to raise funds. We had liquidated all of our assets; sold our house and belongings to make the trip possible.

To help our budget, we stayed in the attic of the church. We spent that first summer sleeping on the church pews to escape heat in the attic. Thankfully an air-conditioner was later installed!

We did everything possible to stretch our budget. When it seemed we'd scraped the bottom of the barrel, God would miraculously provide. At one point we were completely out of food, and God sent someone with $300 worth of groceries to our door.

We worked very hard on that field. We cleaned, mowed, taught Bible studies, and ministered at the mother church and other church plants. We also led weekly evangelistic efforts into the city, conducted youth services, and launched a ministry training program. We were even blessed to plant a new work in the area.

Our time on location was fruitful. We saw many people born again; God added souls to the various works. Our ministry training efforts also blossomed.

Things were going so well we planned to apply as fully appointed missionaries to that nation and serve under the tenured missionary.

Stacey and I were shocked when the missionary returned and, without talking to us, walked to the pulpit and informed the congregation that our season in that nation had come to an end. There was no explanation.

We were hurt and embarrassed. We could not understand what had gone wrong. We were directed by our regional leader to transition to a neighboring country and continue our ministry efforts there.

Our new assignment was to help a national minister plant a church in a major city. The national work had failed three times to plant a church in that city.

When we arrived, we were still wounded over the way we had been dismissed, but we poured ourselves into helping the national pastor plant the new work.

We prayed, fasted, mobilized the nationals in evangelistic work, and held revival services. Once again, God added to the church, and the church began to grow.

Unfortunately, a disagreement arose regarding apostolic doctrine. The national minister we were serving began to reject apostolic truths to the new birth and holiness.

To clarify, I believe strongly that speaking in tongues is the initial evidence of the infilling of the Holy Ghost. Also, speaking in tongues was a critical component of the New Testament believer's daily lives after the initial new-birth experience. I also hold fast to the scriptural fact that without holiness, no man shall see the Lord (Heb. 12:14).

The national minister and his family contended that these doctrines were not biblical absolutes.

Each time someone was filled with the Holy Ghost, their initial experience would be contested and discouraged by the national minister's family. Every church service devolved into a contentious debate.

The tension between me and the national pastor was palpable. We were seldom able to meet without these subjects coming up again.

At some point, the contention became so fierce that we were told we were not allowed to preach, teach, evangelize, or meet with anyone in the city. We were under spiritual house arrest!

We tried every possible avenue to bring resolution and correction to the situation, but nothing seemed to work.

To make matters worse, the national minister called a church meeting (we were given permission to attend) and kicked certain members out of the church. He told them, "As long as you are here, we will not be able to reach wealthy people."

We and the displaced members pleaded with the national minister to reverse the course. There was much weeping, confusion, and great anger in that meeting. Again, after many attempts to resolve the issues, we were left with no other option but to submit to the leadership of the national minister in that nation.

Since we were not permitted to minister in the nation, we returned to the States devastated and confused.

The entire episode was a nightmare of demotions and disappointment. It wasn't long before I received word that the church plant had closed.

A precious woman of God held prayer meetings in her home, trying her very best to keep God's church alive. I am ashamed to say that I took matters into my own hands. Without permission, I returned, rented a community center, contacted all of the people who were previously in the church, and conducted a revival service with them. God filled twelve people with the Holy Ghost that day.

Let me be clear: The outpouring was not God's sanction on my actions but a response to the faith of hungry seekers.

When word of my actions reached leadership, I received a phone call. By this time our profound disappointment had given way to great frustration. The phone call did not go well.

Although we were not asked to resign, we prepared a letter of resignation. At a national conference, I placed the letter in the hand of one our leaders.

I am embarrassed to say that I distinctly remember saying, "If this is how this organization runs, we don't want anything to do with it!"

The leader was as calm and distinguished as ever and simply took my letter of resignation and then said, "Bro. Robinette, what happened to your family was not right. It's terribly wrong. But what you are allowing to happen in you as a result of these wrongs is much worse. You need to get on a plane and wash the feet of those who have wronged you, and maybe God will salvage you and your ministry."

That statement was a wake-up call from the Lord! Spiritual light bulbs flashed in my mind. I knew, without a doubt, I needed to radically humble myself to the missionary who sent me away or my ministry was finished.

I got on an airplane a short time later and flew back to the nation where I had been abruptly dismissed. I met with the missionary privately; we washed each other's feet and prayed together. God gave both of us peace regarding the past.

We still don't know why things happened the way that they did, but we know this is a fact: our negative response to perceived demotion almost killed our ministry.

The demotions exposed flaws in our spiritual armor. Had they not been revealed at that early stage of our ministry, they could have devastated our future.

We were eventually asked to take responsibility for reaching that nation. God restored to us what the locust had eaten. Over the last ten years, God has continued to bless and grow the work.

Whosoever therefore shall humble himself as this little child, the same is greatest in the kingdom of heaven. (Matt. 18:4 KJV)

And whosoever shall exalt himself shall be abased; and he that shall humble himself shall be exalted. (Matt. 23:12 KJV)

Humble yourselves therefore under the mighty hand of God, that he may exalt you in due time. (1 Pet. 5:6 KJV)

If we radically humble ourselves, even when we are wronged, even when we are hurt, or even when it's not fair, God will do a work in us and through us that is beyond our wildest imaginations.

The demotions of others

Briefly, I must add, how we handle the demotion of others also reveals whether we have apprehended the ministry and soul-saving quality of radical humility.

- We should never rejoice in the destruction of God's people.
- We should never celebrate spiritual demotion in God's kingdom.
- We should never relish in ministry failure.
- We should never seek to spiritually harm anyone.
- We should never find excitement in spreading the sensational news of the spiritual or organizational unraveling of God's servants.

The demotion of God's people should bring tears to our eyes, cause our hearts to break and our knees to become worn out from praying for God to restore one that has fallen prey to the enemy!

Restoration (not gossip, criticism, or slander) is our biblical and spiritual responsibility:

Brethren, if a man be overtaken in a fault, ye which are spiritual, restore such an one in the spirit of meekness; considering thyself, lest thou also be tempted. (Gal. 6:1 KJV)

The question "Have you heard what happened to that preacher?" proves one is unspiritual and un-apostolic. Radical humility celebrates the kingdom promotion of others, not their kingdom demotion!

Test 3: Addressing gossip, slander, and criticism directed at you, your family, or your ministry

God has set a high standard of interpersonal ethics for His church. We are not to attack one another. We should never rejoice in gossip, slander, or criticize God's called and anointed vessels. We should never participate in communication that undermines another person. We should never rejoice when someone does not succeed in God's kingdom work.

The Word of God is clear concerning how we should approach our relationship with our fellow brothers and sisters in God's kingdom and their promotion.

In 1 Thessalonians 5:11, the apostle Paul instructed the church to encourage and build one another up in faith and in the work of the kingdom of God.

In Philippians 2:3–4, the apostle Paul articulates the responsibilities we have to our brothers and sisters in Christ in this apostolic kingdom so much clearer:

Let nothing be done through strife or vainglory; but in lowliness of mind let each esteem other better than themselves. Look not every man on his own things, but every man also on the things of others. (Phil. 2:3–4 KJV)

Without a doubt, Hebrews 10:24 should cause conviction to grip our hearts and produce the fruit of righteousness in all of our kingdom relationships:

> And let us consider one another to provoke unto
> love and to good works. (Heb. 10:24 KJV)

Rev. Victor Jackson said, "If you desire to be used of God, be prepared for negative words to come against you. Humble yourself and take the hit.

If you rightly react to hurtful words, the experience will become a refining tool God uses to perfect his instrument.

In 1994, I drove my pastor (who also served as the district superintendent of Michigan) to a district ministers' meeting along with another minister. While driving down the highway, he received a phone call. The moment my pastor answered, a man began to yell, criticize, and slander my pastor. He was yelling so loudly that I could hear his words, even though Pastor Nix's phone was not on speaker phone. My pastor patiently endured the criticism and slander. At the end of the call, he blessed that man in Jesus's name and prayed for him. There was another minister in the back seat of the vehicle, and when my pastor hung up from the call, the other minister exclaimed, "Why didn't you correct that man? He was clearly lying! He was disrespectful! He was unchristian! You should have put him in his place!"

My pastor did not even address the minister in the back seat; he looked at me and said, "Bro. Robinette, if you fight your own battles, God will let you, and you will lose. But if you stand still when you are persecuted by unfair, unchristian, and untrue verbal attacks, God will fight for you. And when God fights for you, you will always win!"

True radical humility does not defend itself. Even Jesus spoke not a word to His accusers at his trial.

Humility takes no thought of human reputations. Human reputation deals with how men perceive us, which seldom has anything to do with how God views us.

True humility has forsaken the entrapping of the pursuit and protection of personal reputation and has fully embraced the pursuit of pleasing God in our motives, thoughts, words, and actions.

One very prominent UPCI leader told me recently, he forbids anyone under his authority to be on the forums where gossip, criticism, and slander proceed unchecked. I personally think that is good practice that all of us should prayerfully consider and employ.

There is great danger when we knowingly and willingly entertain or are entertained by evil communication.

The apostle Paul said,

> Finally, brethren, whatsoever things are true, whatsoever things are honest, whatsoever things are just, whatsoever things are pure, whatsoever things are lovely, whatsoever things are of good report; if there be any virtue, and if there be any praise, think on these things. (Phil. 4:8 KJV)

It is common knowledge that a person can drown in less than sixty seconds when less than one-half cup of water enters their lungs. The same is true when it comes to evil communication. You can spiritually drown in less than sixty seconds when you allow yourself to participate in or be entertained by evil communication. Just one-half cup of evil communication in your spiritual lungs can cause the spiritual man to be corrupted, and spiritual death follows very quickly!

Let me reveal some critical steps that have helped us survive painful, even verbal assaults, and positioned us to thrive in the radically apostolic ministry God called us into:

- Maintain your spiritual disciplines!
- Don't defend yourself!
- Agree with and radically humble yourself before your enemies quickly!

- Take time to honestly and humbly reflect on the attack that is being waged against you and be ready and willing to make necessary changes!
- Stay close to your pastor and let him speak into your life!
- Don't isolate yourself. Remain accessible to your apostolic friends!
- Take time to praise the Lord daily!
- Stay spiritually and purposefully busy in the kingdom of God!

Let these statements sink into your spiritual system:

- The enemy can only destroy us with gossip, slander, and criticism if we allow our prayer life to suffer.
- The enemy can only win if we decide to defend ourselves instead of allowing God to fight for us.
- The enemy is victorious if we take on the same nature of those assaulting us.
- The enemy can only destroy us if we are unwilling to honestly reflect upon the accusations and are resistant to accepting any responsibility.
- The enemy can only hinder our future if we move out from underneath our spiritual authority.
- The enemy can only overcome us if we isolate ourselves.
- The enemy can only stop us if we forget all that God has done for us, and we cease to pray in the storm.
- The enemy can only defeat us if we lay down our calling, vision, and gifting; refusing to minister the way God anointed us to minister in His kingdom.

The journey to becoming radically apostolic is truly challenging at times, but we can make it! Hold on, friend, this painful season shall surely pass, and God will protect the future He planned for you! God will protect the ministry He called you to do! God will protect your family in the midst of the storm!

God will be sure to protect the gifting that He placed in you! As long as you remain radically humble, your future in God's kingdom is secure and unlimited.

The UPCI general superintendent, David K. Bernard, posted the below statement regarding correct communication on a social media platform and listed four principles for God's people to consider:

> As I read some of the comments, I couldn't help but think: Would these ministers want their wife, their children, the young ministers in their church, or their saints to read these comments? Would they approve of saints in their church discussing them on social media in the same way? While we may support the policies of a candidate, we should not adopt the tactics of the world.
>
> Although some will probably accuse me of being naïve, idealistic, and excessively spiritual, I believe that much of what we have observed is worldly, not godly, not according to holiness, and unbecoming to ministers. We need to take a strong stand against these tactics, whether on this forum or elsewhere, and we need to heed the following teachings of Scripture:
>
> - *Be Slow to Speak and Slow to Wrath.* "So then, my beloved brethren, let every man be swift to hear, slow to speak, slow to wrath; for the wrath of man does not produce the righteousness of God" (James 1:19–20 NKJV).
> - *Make Peace.* "But the wisdom that is from above is first pure, then peaceable, gentle, willing to yield, full of mercy and good fruits, without partiality and without hypocrisy. Now the fruit of righteousness is sown in peace by those who make peace" (James 3:17–18 NKJV).

- *Avoid Coarse Jesting.* "But fornication and all uncleanness or covetousness, let it not even be named among you, as is fitting for saints; neither filthiness, nor foolish talking, nor coarse jesting, which are not fitting, but rather giving of thanks" (Ephesians 5:3–4 NKJV).
- *Be Courteous; Don't Revile.* "Finally, all of you be of one mind, having compassion for one another; love as brothers, be tenderhearted, be courteous; not returning evil for evil or reviling for reviling, but on the contrary blessing, knowing that you were called to this, that you may inherit a blessing" (I Peter 3:8–10 NKJV).

5

RADICAL SACRIFICIAL GIVING

Human progress is neither automatic nor inevitable… Every step toward the goal of justice requires sacrifice, suffering, and struggle; the tireless exertions and passionate concern of dedicated individuals.

—*Martin Luther King Jr.*

As base a thing as money often is, yet it can be transmuted into everlasting treasure. It can be converted into food for the hungry and clothing for the poor. It can keep a missionary actively winning lost men to the light of the gospel and thus transmute itself into heavenly values. Any temporal possession can be turned into everlasting wealth. Whatever is given to Christ is immediately touched with immortality.

—*A. W. Tozer*

You can sacrifice and not love. But you cannot love and not sacrifice.

—*Kris Vallotton*

There is that scattereth, and yet increaseth; and there is that withholdeth more than is meet, but it tendeth to poverty. The liberal soul shall be made fat: and he that watereth shall be watered also himself. (Prov. 11:24–25 KJV)

But this I say, He which soweth sparingly shall reap also sparingly; and he which soweth bountifully shall reap also bountifully. Every man according as he purposeth in his heart, so let him give; not grudgingly, or of necessity: for God loveth a cheerful giver. (2 Cor. 9:6–7 KJV)

OUR GIVING STORY

Our revelation of the apostolic power that is born through radical sacrifice giving began in Ypsilanti, Michigan, at the Apostolic Faith Church.

Our pastoral family, Rev. William and Sis. Candace Nix, were among the greatest examples of radical sacrificial givers that we have ever known. Multiple times the Lord blessed the Apostolic Faith Church with seasons of phenomenal growth that required our church to enter into building projects.

On two occasions, Pastor and Sis. Nix stood in the pulpit of the church, and instead of simply asking the body of believers to give sacrificially, they exampled it. I will never forget when they announced they would surrender their retirement funds so we could build a new church. I never witnessed anything like that before or since. Bro. and Sis. Nix's example planted the seed of sacrificial giving in our spiritual systems that has produced immeasurable amounts of fruit over our twenty-six years of apostolic ministry. We have also learned that when we sacrifice for God, we cannot out-give God.

The Ypsilanti, Michigan, church was greatly blessed because our church family followed the example of our pastoral family. We enjoyed favor and increase in our churches finances, evangelism efforts, and ministries. We continually witnessed the fruit promised in Malachi 3:10–12 and Luke 6:38.

In August of 1994, when we were first married, we made the commitment to radical sacrificial giving as a family. We were young and poor, but we wanted to establish the pattern and practice of sacrificial giving in our family finances at the beginning of our beautiful journey as a married couple. I was nineteen years old, and Stacey had just turned eighteen when we first began partnering with global missionary families. We didn't have much of anything, but we purposed every single month to give sacrificially to those who were actively attempting to reach the world. We did not own hardly any furniture when we first got married. We actually only owned a twin-size bed and a few small bedroom items. We were living in Germany at the time, and during a certain season, the German people would put all the things they did not want out on the curb. The Americans called it German junking. It was often really good items. I can't even tell you how many wonderful things God blessed us with while we drove around those German towns during the German junking season. We attended Bethel United Pentecostal Church in Landstuhl, Germany, at the time. There was a large furniture directly underneath the church, and we used their parking lot to park our cars during our church services. One evening when we came to the church, we noticed there was a beautiful, five-piece, white leather, living room furniture set sitting in the parking lot near the curb of the street. My wife said, "That's our blessing! That's probably German junking. Let's go get that."

I told her, "Baby, that is not our blessing. Look how beautiful and new that looks. There is no way that is German junking." Well, after further discourse followed by a rather uncomfortable and convincing season of silence, we walked into the furniture store and asked for the manager. I said, "Sir, we have been giving to missions, and we saw that furniture outside, and *my wife* thinks that's our blessings. Is that German junking, and can we just take that?" The manager started laughing and proceeded to explain to me that the furniture outside was brand new and was valued at five thousand deutsche marks. They were clearing a space in the middle of the store to make that white leather set of furniture the centerpiece of their store. I of course was thoroughly embarrassed and apologized to the manager for wasting his time and proceeded to usher my wife out of the store. Then the manager said, "Wait a moment. Are you really missions givers, and did you really believe that was your blessing?"

We said, "Yes, sir."

He said, "Then we will give it to you free of charge. Give us your address and we will personally deliver all five pieces to your home tomorrow."

You just can't out-give God!

On Friday night, September 30, 2005, during the UPCI General Conference, the late apostle, Rev. Steve Willoughby, was preaching the foreign missions' service. Forgive me, I do not remember what he preached, but I will never forget what he imparted. At the end of that service, Bro. Willoughby took a check for $10,000 out of his pocket and said the Lord told him to give it in the foreign missions' offering that evening. Faith was very high in that service. In those years, all of the appointed foreign missionaries attending general conference sat on the platform during their department's service. While Bro. Willoughby made the appeal to the general conference assembly to join him in radical sacrifice, God spoke to me and said, "What are you waiting for? Make a pledge for $10,000 and prove me this day if I will not open the windows of heaven for you and give you blessings that you will not have room to receive."

We did not have $10,000. As a matter of fact, we didn't even have $100 in the bank! But God had spoken, and I wanted to obey God! My wife was not on the platform with me, but I was certain that she was feeling the same thing that I was feeling, but just in case, I tried to call her from the platform to confirm we were in one mind and one accord. What I didn't know was my wife was trying to call me from her balcony seat at the same time to tell me that what I was feeling was *not* God! Since I could not reach her, I assumed that her silence was confirmation that we were in unity about making a pledge of $10,000. I found a piece of paper and wrote, "The Robinette family will give $10,000. Just give us some time to get it."

I came off the platform with tears streaming down my face with joy at the prospect of proving God, but my wife met me in the altar with tears streaming down her face because she did not reach me in time to stop my leap of madness. While we stood in the altar weeping for different reasons, a minister walked up behind us and reached around me and put a check in my left front suit pocket without saying a word. I was too busy weeping to realize the miracle of the moment. I had forgotten all about the check in my pocket until we arrived at our hotel that evening. When I emptied the contents of my pockets onto the desk in the hotel room, I found the check. When I opened the folded check, it was for $20,000!!! There was a note with the check that said, "You proved God and He proved you can never out-give him!"

We wept like little babies in the hotel room that night and rejoiced in the faithfulness of our great God!

UPCI Foreign Missions reported the results of that service like this:

> Men and women, pastors and businesses, united tonight to give a record cash offering of over $1.1 million as well as Partner in Missions (PIM) support of over $1 million. Because of the generous giving from the United Pentecostal Church, ten missionary families will have the privilege of returning to the field from the General Conference. They will not need to deputize to raise funds one more day. In addition to this miraculous show of Kingdom giving, the men and women of the UPCI pledged and gave over $1.1 million to help erase deficits and provide reserve funds for our traveling missionaries. Those who pledged and gave $500 and above were given glow-sticks. When arena staff turned off the house lights, hundreds of glow-sticks pierced the darkness and the woes of deputation in an overwhelming show of support and solidarity for our foreign missionaries. To all those who gave…to those who sacrificed…to those who will give… Thank you!

That experience has been a catalyst for continued and consistent sacrificial giving in our ministry and has returned unto us blessings beyond our wildest imaginations!

We continued the example of sacrificial giving when we became pastor of the United Pentecostal Church in Vienna, Austria, which we later renamed Church of Acts.

Over the eleven years we pastored there, our family personally sponsored twenty-one missionary families and gave well over $1,000 each month to UPCI Global Missions and to missionary efforts to the German-speaking nations.

The Church of Acts congregation followed our example and also began to give sacrificially, both globally and locally, to facilitate God's unprecedented global harvest.

In April of 2008, we held our first Faith Promise revival in Austria. Faith Promise is a program for local churches to secure pledges from their congregations to financially support missionary efforts around the world. We invited two missionaries and a Global Missions representative from our fellowship to attend.

Prior to that weekend, our church did not give regularly to missions, but thanks to the sacrifice of God's people, the Church of Acts began giving over €2,000 ($2,940) a month to missionary efforts around the world. Over the final three years of our pastorate, the church gave €200,000 ($236,000) to missions.

The decision to begin our pastorate with sacrificial giving was one of the keys that unlocked unprecedented harvest and many mighty miracles in the nation of Austria.

We continued to practice the call to radical sacrificial giving in our personal giving even after we left the pastorate of the Church of Acts in Vienna, Austria.

On September 27, 2017, while preaching the UPCI General Conference Global Mission service, we were planning to give $10,000 again in that Global Missions' offering as we had many times before. But while I was preaching, the Lord spoke to me and said, "If you keep giving the same amount of radical sacrifice, you will continue to witness the same level of blessing, but if you will double your offering, I will double your blessings!"

Once again, without counseling with my precious wife, Stacey, I stood in the pulpit and said, "God just told us to give $20,000 in this offering."

My wife and I had previously agreed to make a $10,000 pledge during the service, and she was standing in the altar with an additional $20 bill in her hand to give in the cash offering. When she heard me say we were now giving $20,000, she put the $20 bill back in her purse and told Missionary Tanya Harrod, "I'm keeping that $20 because we're going to need it!"

General director of UPCI Global Missions, Rev. Bruce Howell, sent the following text message after the service:

"Offering total $2,373,616.00…cash—$608,983.00…fifteen missionaries will be sent back (to the field). Already advised five! Bruce Howell and GM."

I wish that I could report to you that someone came up to me and put a $20,000 check in my pocket, but it did not happen like that.

A little over one month later, I was back in my office in Vienna, Austria, prior to a Sunday morning service. There was a letter from our Global Missions director, Rev. Bruce Howell, giving a friendly reminder to pay pledges before the end of the year.

To be honest, I became a bit stressed. We did not have $20,000, and I did not know how we would pay that large of a pledge before Christmas. I thought to myself, *I'll just bring this to the Church of Acts' saints today and see if we can make this a church project. Then we can certainly pay this off in a one month.*

I sat in my office chair and reminded God of what He spoke to me in that pulpit at UPCI General Conference on September 27, 2017. I placed the letter from Rev. Bruce Howell on the side of my desk to carry to the pulpit, and I opened the next letter in my mail packet. When I opened the letter, a check fell out—it was for $20,000!

I began to weep! God had done it again! You just cannot outgive God! I took that check and Bro. Howell's letter to the pulpit that morning and told the church what God had done. Wow! We had *church* that Sunday!

Our family's financial dream is to one day be able to financially partner with every UPCI missionary. We are not afraid of radical sacrificial giving, and we believe God will position us to be a financial blessing to His global church in these last days.

Let me share with you some more powerful testimonies of radical sacrifice from ministers and saints:

*****

Jill and I were newlyweds serving as music ministers in North Carolina, USA. We didn't have much, but we believed in giving, and we believed in missions. We did not give to receive, but we believed the promises pertaining to God's favor for givers.

On a Wednesday night, a young missionary couple, Charles and Stacey Robinette, came to our church and shared their heart and burden for their calling to Global Missions. We could really feel their passion. As they spoke to our congregation, God began to speak to my wife and me to support their ministry. We both felt led to give sacrificially.

I was playing the piano, and my wife was praying in the altar. We exchanged glances, and we could sense that God was speaking identically to us both to give everything! My wife made her way to where I was at the piano and whispered in my ear what she felt that God said to her. I told her that I was feeling exactly the same thing. We did not have very much at all, but we gave all that we had in our bank account. We wrote the check and took a deep breath. We believed that God would take care of us, but we were still a little nervous.

The weatherman was calling for a snowstorm to pass through that night. After church, we gathered up the loose change from our car and found the little bit of cash we had left. We went to the store for some essentials, just in case we were to be snowed in for a few days. Driving home, as we approached our apartment in the evangelist quarters of the church, our old car just died. It had served us well since my college days, but it literally shut off completely as we were driving. We coasted silently into the parking lot of the church and that was the end of that ride. Neither of us wanted to say what was going through both of our minds at the time.

We sat quietly, staring straight ahead in silence while watching the snow fall for a few minutes. I looked over at my wife and said, "God is going to take care of us." I don't know if I really believed it, but it seemed like the right thing to say at the time! Little did we know, that for a few weeks before any of this happened, God had been speaking to a family to buy us a car. Several family members, without consulting with each other, had been led by the Lord to buy us a new vehicle. In the days that followed, this family notified us of their plans. We wept as they shared what God had placed in their hearts. They wept as we told them of the missions offering that God encouraged us to give.

Within a few days, we were handed the keys to a fully loaded car that we would have never been able to afford on our own. Back then, I am not sure too many people had heard of Charles Robinette. God gave us a miracle, and He privileged us to invest in the many miracles that have happened around the world through the ministry of the Robinette family.

Rev. Brian and Jill Careccia
Music Ministers
Heavenview UPC, Winston Salem, NC

*****

Missionary Charles Robinette delivered a message at our evening service that confirmed what the Lord had placed on my heart recently. I gave in the offerings the night that Missionary Robinette spoke, but most importantly, I made up in my mind that I was going to surrender my finances to Christ. This included my regular tithes and offerings, donating to other ministries within the church, and changing my mindset about the money I give. My mind had to be resolute. When I prayed, I asked God to make me a cheerful giver. I asked God to bring people my way so that I could bless them. I prayed that the Lord would increase my faith as I paid my tithes and offerings. And most importantly, when I prayed, I continually thanked God for what He was going to do in my life.

No less than a week later, the blessing started pouring in! I was told I was getting a bonus at work. They told me it was not going to be a very large bonus, but I was grateful anyways. I thought I was going to be receiving a $25 gift card; instead, I was handed a bonus check of $300! I was so happy, and then I remembered...that God is faithful to His promises.

That very same weekend, I went home to visit my parents. They blessed me with an additional $100! I couldn't wait to get back to Tampa to tithe on my blessing and bless my younger brother! But it doesn't end there! I really did change my mindset about giving. At this point, I know that God is going to provide for me, and I stopped worrying about it. I really simply stopped worrying about the financial pressures of student loans, the car note, and the rent.

On September 2, I was promoted to supervisor at my agency! I had applied for the position three to four weeks prior and had not heard anything from anyone in regards to the position. I was starting to think that I was not going to get the position, but then I remembered that God is the one that will promote me, not man. The blessings have been pouring in, and I am truly grateful to God for keeping me.

Angelina Adams

*****

- A man in Louisiana bought a piece of property and was making payments when the bank called in the loan. He owed $100,000 by Monday morning or the property would be forfeited to the bank. By Sunday of the Faith Promise service, he had only come up with $50,000 cash that he could give to the bank, but he was still $50,000 short. During the Faith Promise service, he decided since he couldn't save the property, so he would give all $50,000 to missions. Monday he showed up at the bank to let them know he was going to default. The manager immediately came out and shook his hand and said, "Thank you for paying your loan in full." He said, "Please check your records again. I didn't pay you anything. I came to let you know that I don't have the money to pay you." The bank manager let him know that on Sunday at the same time of his church service where he gave $50,000 to missions, a payment of $100,000 was posted on the loan!

- On 8/10/14 during the revival service, my husband and I felt led to give during the evening service through the faith giving message that was being preached by Rev. Robinette. We gave our paycheck we had in hand knowing that we needed that paycheck to pay the mortgage. By faith we signed it over and placed it in the offering bucket. God not only made a way to pay the mortgage, but we got a call on Tuesday, 8/12/14, that we would receive a check for $10,000.00. *Praise God*! The blessings did not stop there. Somehow our credit card bill ended up at another address a few days later, and we got a call that it was not only paid in full, it was overpaid. God kept pouring out the blessing. We were blessed with stack of brand-new clothes for our entire family. And the blessings continued. On August 30, someone blessed us with a brand-new 2014 vehicle for $25,000 *paid in cash* with no payments. The blessings of the Lord maketh rich and addeth no sorrow to it. To God be the glory for the great things He has done. We have proven that you cannot out-give God. Thank you, Jesus!
- Richard gave sacrificially during the service on 8/10/14. On his first semester, they gave him $138.00 back, and his $9,000.00 tuition is paid for the year. He put the $138.00 they gave him toward the second semester, and he only paid $68.00 for his senior year of college. He received a scholarship, work study, and worked camp meetings but did not expect this low of a payment.
- ❖ The Lord instructed me to give a sacrificial offering during the missions conference with Rev. Robinette. I gave what

cash I had on me at the time and emptied out my bank accounts. Then the Lord told me to give my electronic items as well, so I did. In a short week, I was blessed with a brand-new 2015 Kia car. This was a miracle because I have bad credit, and I was able to get a low APR. To God be the glory.

Bishop Daniel Davy
Testimonies from New Life Tabernacle, Seffner, FL

*****

When I was pastoring in Jacksonville, NC, Bro. Robinette visited and shared the needs of German-speaking nations in Europe and the vision his family had. A young man that was preparing to join the military at the time came to my office after service with tears in his eyes and asked if he could speak with me. He said, "Pastor, I need some guidance. I am nearly overwhelmed with a burden to do something to support this missionary."

I said, "Well, good—what's the problem?"

He said, "Well, the only money I have is the money I have been saving under my mattress to buy a motorcycle, and I think God is telling me to give that."

I let him know I couldn't make that decision for him, but that I have learned over the years that you just can't out-give God, and many times when He asks something like this of you, He's preparing you for a blessing! Well, he gave that money—all of it! And since then, God has blessed him with a new home, a new truck, a wife, and a child! He was actually one of the young men who helped me start Richlands UPC!"

Pastor Matthew Drake
Jacksonville, NC

*****

I pray that today, as you have read the testimonies of our Lord, you will allow the Holy Ghost to transform you, your heart, your mind, and your sacrificial giving!

The word of God is filled with testimonies and examples of radical sacrificial giving:

In 1 Kings 17:13, it shares the story of the widow at Zarephath. She first made the prophet Elijah a cake with everything she had left. God responded to her radical sacrificial giving, and He didn't just meet her immediate needs, but her blessing flowed over. God gave her enough oil and meal for her and her son to thrive in the midst of the season of drought.

Matthew 26:7–13 gives us a glimpse into another example of radical sacrificial giving. A woman with an alabaster box of very precious ointment pours it on the head of Jesus. The disciples saw it as waste, but Jesus called it a good work! Jesus declared that her sacrifice would be a memorial of her. That is truly amazing!

When you read Luke 21, you get an even clearer picture of how Jesus views our offerings. The Bible says the rich men were casting their gifts into the offering plate. They were giving out of their abundance. But a certain poor widow woman gave two mites. Two mites together were the equivalent of the smallest Roman coin. Those who were simply giving out of their abundance did not solicit a response from Jesus, but when the widow woman gave, as the Bible says, all the living that she had, Jesus responded, "Of a truth I say unto you, that this poor widow hath cast in more than they all."

Let's not forget the fact that in Acts 2:44 and Acts 4:32, the early church sold all their possessions and lands and gave to those who had needs.

One of the passages of scripture that reinforce this valuable principle of radical sacrificial giving is 2 Corinthians 8:2 (ESV):

> For in a severe test of affliction, their abundance
> of joy and their extreme poverty have overflowed
> in a wealth of generosity on their part.

The Macedonian Church, who was poverty stricken, radically gave sacrificially, beyond their ability. They were not obsessed with laying up personal treasures, acquiring personal wealth, or even meeting their own personal needs; they gave sacrificially to others and trusted that God would bless them, pressed down, shaken together, and running over.

In Matthew 7:11, we have a promise from God that will never fail:

> If ye then, being evil, know how to give good gifts unto your children, how much more shall your Father which is in heaven give good things to them that ask him? Therefore all things whatsoever ye would that men should do to you, do ye even so to them: for this is the law and the prophets. (Matt. 7:11–12 KJV)

God will bless you as you bless others and as you give to facilitate His kingdom vision!

You can't out-give God!

The Bible gives clarity to how we ought to give:

- We should give cheerfully (2 Cor. 9:7)!
- Our giving should be motivated by love (1 Cor. 13:3)!
- We should honor God with firstfruits of our wealth (Prov. 3:9)!
- We should give with a right spirit (Matt. 6:2)!
- We should give to anyone who ask (Luke 6:30)
- We should give generously (Prov. 3:27)

Take a look at some of the promises associated with radically sacrificial giving:

- It will be well with the person who gives generously (Ps. 112:5)!
- You will be blessed if you give bountifully (Prov. 22:9)!

- Your children will be blessed because of your generosity (Ps. 37:26)
- The work of your hands will be blessed (Prov. 3:9 and Prov. 11:25)!
- You will be happy if you are generous (Acts 20:35)
- You grow richer (Prov. 11:24)!
- God himself will meet your needs (Phil. 4:19 and Prov. 28:27)!

The promises of God associated with radical sacrificial giving are too great to list in this book and too certain for His church to reject.

Let me speak into your spiritual systems:

- No more fear!
- No more holding back our finances from the Lord!
- No more hesitation!
- No more simply giving out of our abundance!

We, God's radically apostolic church, are going to make the power-producing, apostolic shift to the faith-filled discipline of radical sacrificial giving!

We cannot wait to hear the testimonies of the financial miracles that God is going to give to you as you radically sacrifice for the kingdom of our great God!

6

RADICAL APOSTOLIC REALITY

*God has privileged us in Christ Jesus to live above the ordinary
human plane of life. Those who want to be ordinary and live
on a lower plane can do so, but as for me, I will not.*

—Smith Wigglesworth

*I can say, through the power of the Spirit that wherever
God can get a people that will come together in one accord
and one mind in the Word of God, the baptism of the Holy
Ghost will fall upon them, like as at Cornelius' house.*

—William J. Seymour

*The purpose of a spirit filled life is to demonstrate the supernatural
power of our living God so that the unsaved multitudes will abandon
their dead gods to call upon the name of The Lord and be delivered.*

—T. L. Osborn

And my speech and my preaching was not with enticing words of man's wisdom, but in demonstration of the Spirit and of power: That your faith should not stand in the wisdom of men, but in the power of God. (1 Cor. 2:4–5 KJV)

In these last days, we are witnessing an unprecedented demonstration of the power of God in churches, cities, and nations all around the world!

I have been privileged to see many incredible outpourings of the Holy Ghost and thousands of miracles around the world. I've witnessed God's power breaking into religious institutions, overtaking political opposition, and erasing social barriers!

Let me share some of the testimonies of the baptism of the Spirit of the God that we have recently witnessed around the globe:

- In Manila, God filled at least eight thousand people with the Holy Ghost in one meeting!
- In Bangladesh, God filled over seven thousand people with the Holy Ghost in one meeting, and there were reports of over seven thousand miracles!
- In Pakistan, God filled over three hundred people with the Holy Ghost in one meeting!
- In Madagascar, God filled at least one thousand seven hundred people with the Holy Ghost in one meeting!
- In Malawi, God filled at least three thousand people with the Holy Ghost during the crusade weekend!
- In Guatemala, God filled about eight hundred fifty-eight people with the Holy Ghost in one meeting!
- In Thailand, God filled two hundred eighty-four people with the Holy Ghost in one meeting!
- In Haiti, God filled five hundred eighty-four people with the Holy Ghost in one meeting!
- In Mindanao, God filled one thousand five hundred fifty-five people with the Holy Ghost in one meeting!

In addition to these great outpourings of the Spirit of the Lord, we have seen entire trinitarian organizations receiving the revelation of the mighty God in Christ, being rebaptized in the name of Jesus, and being filled with the Holy Ghost.

In March 2020, during the COVID-19 pandemic, we received a phone call from a pastor in Duisburg, Germany. He told us we needed to visit a Romanian Pentecostal church in Essen, Germany.

On March 1, 2020, my family drove to Essen to meet with Pastor Cantemir Floarea. We found the church to be loving, generous, and passionate. I preached that night about the power of the name of Jesus.

Every Romanian in the building crowded the altar, weeping, calling on the name of Jesus, and many were filled with the Holy Ghost, speaking with other tongues, just like the Bible records.

Following that service, Pastor Floarea asked us to return on March 12, 2020, to preach in another Romanian Pentecostal church in Gelsenkirchen, Germany.

I returned with my family along with Bro. and Sis. Nathan Hulsman, missionaries to Switzerland. The church was packed with men, women, and children who were hungry for the demonstration and power of our mighty God.

The Holy Ghost fell when at the conclusion of service. God filled thirty-six of those precious people with the Holy Ghost; over fifty people reported notable miracles.

As of this book's writing, we are coordinating with the churches in Essen and Gelsenkirchen to rebaptize their members in Jesus's name. This is apostolic reality!

We need to transition from the thinking that revival is coming to revival is here!

The revelation of baptism in Jesus's name is sweeping through the nations! The Holy Ghost is being poured in nations that have long been closed to Christianity! The whole earth is being filled with the glory of the Lord! No one and nothing can stop what God is doing in these last days!

The Lord has been speaking to me about the need for the church to resist the spirit of fear! We are inundated with information that is stoking fear in our hearts. Mainstream news outlets shamelessly sow seeds of panic and dread every day.

Social media giants and political entities are saturating the nation with false narratives about pandemics, the economy, and social issues. It's a time where Jesus promised in Luke 21:26 that men's hearts would fail them because of fear because of what is happening in the world.

In Matthew 6 and Mark 13, Jesus commanded:

- Don't be fearful about your life!
- Don't be fearful about what you're going to eat and drink!
- Don't be fearful of your needs!
- Don't be fearful concerning tomorrow!
- Don't be fearful about what you will say!

> Behold the fowls of the air: for they sow not, neither do they reap, nor gather into barns; yet your heavenly Father feedeth them. Are ye not much better than they? (Matt. 6:26 KJV)

> And why take ye thought for raiment? Consider the lilies of the field, how they grow; they toil not, neither do they spin: And yet I say unto you, That even Solomon in all his glory was not arrayed like one of these. Wherefore, if God so clothe the grass of the field, which today is, and tomorrow is cast into the oven, shall he not much more clothe you, O ye of little faith? (Matt. 6:28–30 KJV)

We do not have to fall prey to the pandemic of fear in our world! We are not ordinary men and women! We are the radically apostolic church that has been born again of the water and the Spirit!

I am not saying that every concern or problem is imagined. Many of our world's challenges are irrefutably real. But even the reality of crisis and chaos is secondary to the reality of God and His church. We must attach our faith to the apostolic reality of God's power and His promises to the church in the last days.

> But seek ye first the kingdom of God, and his righteousness; and all these things shall be added unto you. (Matt. 6:33 KJV)

Which reality are you obsessing over, the kingdom of this world or the kingdom of God? I'm not espousing that you should ignore this present world, but I am reminding you to seek God's kingdom first. If the most important facts in your life are from mainstream media, it will hold your ministry hostage. If the most important facts come from the Bible, it will release your ministry.

Paul warns us in Colossians 3:2 to set our affections on things above, not on things of this world. Choose which reality you will live by. Choose to feed your faith, not your fears.

If your life mantra is that the world is bad and getting worse, you're not wrong. If you choose to believe that God is good and He is at work, you're not wrong. Choose your reality.

We cannot allow fear to infect God's global church. We cannot allow fear to affect the way we minister to God's people. We cannot allow fear to change the way we operate in our biblical apostolic ministries.

We must not forget our "apostolic reality" that Paul declared:

> For God hath not given us the spirit of fear; but of power, and of love, and of a sound mind. (2 Tim. 1:7 KJV)

If God did not give you fear, it cannot stay!

If fear did not come from the Lord, it has no place in your life!

We have an apostolic reality that is certain, regardless of what is happening in the world.

Our "apostolic reality" is that we have the power to

- see the dead raised to life again (John 11:38–44, Mark 7:8–11, and Acts 9),
- cause the blind to see (John 9:1–7, Matt. 9:27–31, Mark 8:22–26, and Mark 18:35–43),
- make the deaf to hear (Mark 7:31–37),
- cause diseases to be miraculously healed (Mark 17:11–19),
- speak the word of faith and creative miracles will manifest (Mark 22:50–51), and
- lay hands on those who are crippled and they will walk (Acts 3:2–11)!

God's demonstration and power is our "apostolic reality!"

> But ye shall receive power, after that the Holy Ghost is come upon you. (Acts 1:8 KJV)

> He gave them power against unclean spirits, to cast them out, and to heal all manner of sickness and all manner of disease. (Matt. 10:1 KJV)

> And these signs shall follow them that believe; In my name shall they cast out devils; they shall speak with new tongues; They shall take up serpents; and if they drink any deadly thing, it shall not hurt them; they shall lay hands on the sick, and they shall recover. (Mark 16:17–18 KJV)

The "apostolic reality" is that God's apostolic church is the solution to every global pandemic and societal breakdown!

Jesus promised His church:

> Verily, verily, I say unto you, He that believeth on me, the works that I do shall he do also; and greater works than these shall he do; because I go unto my Father. And whatsoever ye shall ask in my name, that will I do, that the Father may be

glorified in the Son. If ye shall ask any thing in
my name, I will do it. (John 14:12–14 KJV)

In Acts 4:33, the apostles testified of the resurrection of Jesus with great power!

In Acts 6:8, Stephen was full of faith and power. He did great wonders and miracles!

Our "apostolic reality" is that we have the demonstration and power of the Holy Ghost flowing through our spiritual veins. We ought to speak, lead, and act as if we have the power of God inside of us!

God is positioning His radically apostolic church all over the globe so that we can see and accomplish His vision of global harvest in these last days!

Let me declare some things into your spiritual system:

- It's time for this radically apostolic army to pull down the strongholds of fear that are plaguing our lives, ministries, cities, and nations!
- It's time to cast down the fearful imaginations that are limiting kingdom potential!
- The spirit of fear has arrogantly exalted itself!
- But the radically apostolic church is going to break the back of fear, right now, in Jesus's name!
- We are going awaken to our "apostolic reality!"
- We are not going to entertain what the enemy and the world has given to us.
- We are going to celebrate and exalt in our hearts, in our minds, in our faith, and in our spirits the things that God himself has given unto us!
- We must boldly preach the Word of God!
- We must boldly lay hands on the sick, and they shall recover!
- We must boldly speak the word of faith!
- We must boldly baptize the masses by immersion in the only saving name of Jesus!

- We must boldly pray people through to the Holy Ghost!
- We must boldly carry the gospel to the entire world!

Why are you reading this book? Maybe it is for information or inspiration, but I will guess that you are feeling the call of God to be radically apostolic.

Maybe you are expecting apostolic impartation of the Spirit of the Lord.

I declare demonstration of the Spirit and power of the Almighty God are yours in Jesus's name! You are going to be mightily used of God in these last days!

God will use you to make a global impact before the trumpet sounds! Let me pray the prayer of faith over you right now: "By the authority of the Word of God, by the power of the name of Jesus, and by the power of the Holy Ghost that is falling upon you as you read these words, a supernatural anointing is being imparted and released upon you right now, in Jesus's name! A baptism of radically apostolic demonstration and power of the Holy Ghost is coming upon your leadership and your ministry right now, in the name of Jesus! A radically apostolic boldness and authority is coming upon you right now, in Jesus's name! A radically apostolic gift of faith is coming upon you right now, in Jesus's name!"

Lift up your hands, and celebrate what God is baptizing you with right now!

7

RADICAL TESTIMONIES

While writing this book, I realized that the Lord had given us multitudes of testimonies that I simply could not thread into the chapters, but they needed to be told.

What you are about to read will prove that the power of God is working in our generation.

Miracles and Holy Ghost outpourings are not relics of the past; they are happening right now, all over the world.

I pray these testimonies will serve as a strong boost to your faith and will encourage you to step out in boldness so that you can see the outpouring of the Holy Ghost and miracles with your own eyes!

*****

On the doorstep of the United States sits the poorest country in the western hemisphere, Haiti. With only 10,714 square miles and an estimated 10.8 million people, Haiti is a place of darkness, severe poverty, and despair. You won't find many cruise ships or crowds of tourists, just numerous conclaves of voodoo and demonic worship. It is not a popular site for destination weddings. It is a place of hurt and distrust. It is a place where needs far outweigh satisfaction. Hope is a distant dream, and pain is a daily reminder. Haiti is a desperate mission field.

Recently, we were returning late at night from our crusade site in Saint-Marc, Haiti, to our hotel. We kept encountering one roadblock after another as armed bandits hiding in the darkness were barricading the roads so vehicles could not pass. We passed through three different barricades without incident but eventually came up to a roadblock of boulders and concrete obstructions that we could not pass. Jordan, our friend and security guard, who also protects the president of Haiti, was riding next to me in a convoy of four vans. He ordered the vehicle to stop and for everyone to remain in the vans. Jordan approached the barricade with his nine-millimeter pistol drawn. He started to remove the obstruction when shots rang out. The dust from bullets hitting the boulders around Jordan sprayed in the air as Jordan ducked and weaved while returning fire and moving boulders. The bullets and large rocks were coming at all of us from both sides of the street. The black backdrop of night and the gunfire revealed we were in an ambush!

Somehow, Jordan was able to move enough of the roadblock obstacles so we could pass. All four vans passed without anyone being shot or hurt. When we arrived at our hotel, Jordan told us that he saw shields surrounding our vehicles when he looked back at the vans. God was protecting His people! Jordan received the Holy Ghost in the crusade and gave all the glory to God. There were also another 536 people that God filled with his Spirit, and over two hundred reported notable miracles. For many, the story ends there, but not for apostolic Pentecostals that believe everyone should hear the truth.

Pastor David E. Myers
Eastwind Pentecostal Church
Palm Bay, FL

*****

In 2008, the Malawi A-Team, which included our team leader, Bishop Daniel Garlitz, Rev. Charles Wright, Rev. Greg Hurley, Rev. David Bounds, Rev. Robert Gordon, and myself, conducted our first crusade in the city of Lilongwe, Malawi.

We had high faith and invested a significant amount financially to facilitate a great crusade in the nation of Malawi. Upon arrival, the event was not organized or advertised as well as we had been told. Rev. David Bounds articulated it correctly when he said, "We were expecting ten thousand people, but only three hundred fifty attended the meeting."

Amazingly, God filled three hundred thirty-six with the Holy Ghost, and forty-four were baptized in Jesus's name in spite of all the challenges and meager attendance.

Following that first crusade, we began working together with the national church leaders to prepare them for greater harvest in the nation of Malawi.

To give you an understanding of some of the challenges we were experiencing in the beginning of the A-Team efforts in Malawi, let me share with you another miracle.

While facilitating an altar worker training seminar in Malawi, it became evident that none of the one hundred plus national ministry team members had ever received the Holy Ghost. Some seemed confused about what we were teaching; others were outright resistant.

I leaned over to Bishop Garlitz and said, "I don't think any of these ministers have the Holy Ghost and have spoken with other tongues."

Bishop Garlitz said, "No, these are Malawian preachers. Their wives and the ministry team members are from their local churches."

The longer we taught, the more obvious the doctrinal and spiritual disconnect became clear.

At some point, Bishop Garlitz leaned over to me and said, "Do whatever you feel to do in the Holy Ghost."

When I took the pulpit, I asked everyone to stand who had never received the Holy Ghost and spoken with other tongues like the Bible says. Almost the entire room stood up. So we asked them to sit down, and we asked them again to make sure they did not misunderstand us. Again, almost everyone in the room stood! Preachers and ministers all stood to receive the Holy Ghost! We led them into a prayer of repentance, and when we started to speak the word of faith, the electricity went off (as it always does in Malawi), and we lost the sound system and the lights at the same time. The room was completely dark. You couldn't see anything in front of you at all.

We spoke the word of faith as loud as we could! With no microphone and no lights! Then a spiritual wind and a great sound from heaven broke loose in the darkness! It sounded like water was rushing through the room. Then the lights came back on, and everyone in the room was weeping and speaking with other tongues!

This was obviously a catalyst moment for the nation of Malawi.

As the training and spiritual maturity of the field began to increase, God began to do an unprecedented work in the nation of Malawi.

From the first crusade in 2008 to the last Malawi A-Team crusade in 2017, we witnessed God fill at least 10,665 with the gift of the Holy Ghost, at least 1,440 baptized in Jesus's name, at least 192 blind people received their sight, at least 83 deaf people received their hearing, at least 75 people who had visible tumors watched as they disappeared by the power of the Almighty God, at least 1,167 testified of being miraculously healed of all manner of diseases, and at least 15 who were brought in to the crusade services crippled left completely whole!

Missionary Charles G. Robinette
General Superintendent of Germany,
Switzerland, Liechtenstein, and Austria

*****

While ministering in Lilongwe, a man who was possessed with devils tried to attack me during the preaching. When he came toward me, he stopped about halfway to the pulpit because it looked like he was fistfighting something or someone. He was swinging his arms like he was under attack by invisible bees. None of us were prepared for what happened next. Something picked that man up and threw him almost twenty feet in the air and struck a brick wall. When he hit the wall, he broke his leg. We were astonished!

The elders from the crusade and security team brought him to the altar. God miraculously healed his leg! He went home with a miracle. He brought his family back, and all three received the gift of the Holy Ghost and were baptized in Jesus's name.

During one of our early A-Team crusades when the local administration and organization was not fully developed, we arrived on the crusade grounds only to find nobody was there except us and a national representative. The entire field was empty except for a gathering of witch doctors (I believe they were called Zionists) that built a fire on the edge of the crusade field. Those witch doctors were completely possessed of devils. When our team arrived, the smoke from their fire was covering the soccer field. They were burning plastic and corn silk to shut down the crusade. We all got out of the vehicle. We began to pray that God would allow the wind to change directions and blow the smoke toward the marketplace because the smoke was blowing directly into our faces. As soon as we all prayed, the wind changed directions immediately! It blew all of the smoke off the soccer field and into the marketplace. The witch doctors were still casting spells and cursing the A-Team members. The witch doctors had large black snakes that they were dancing with and swinging above their heads. Due to the witch doctors' presence and fear of their curses, the Malawian people were too afraid to gather on the field. Even the national leader recommended that we leave and have no service that evening. Bro. Robinette and I, with a translator, left the platform and began walking across the field, shouting the name of Jesus at those witch doctors! When we began rebuking them, the translator began to declare everything we were saying in Chichewa. Those witch doctors began to become even more agitated. One got so angry that he put the head of the black snake in his mouth; the tail of the snake was wrapping around his head. The witch doctor began chanting with the snake head in his mouth, and his eyes began to roll back until you could only see the whites of his eyes. We just continued to plead the blood of Jesus! When the witch doctor perceived we were not afraid of him and that his spells and curses were not working, he took the snake by the tail and began trying to throw the snake on Bro. Robinette and me. We just stood there pleading the blood of Jesus. At some point, the witch doctors fled the field in fear of our God! As soon as the shenanigans were concluded and the Malawian people saw what our God did to the witch doctors, they gathered in great numbers that evening, and multitudes were filled with the Holy Ghost and baptized in Jesus's name! Many Malawians who were possessed with devils were delivered that night during the crusade service.

Another powerful experience happened in Lilongwe. While ministering, the nationals were carrying crippled men into the crusade on the carts. They placed them to the right of the platform probably one hundred yards away. They set them down so they can hear the preaching of the word of God. After we preached about repentance, faith in God, and then spoke the word of faith, those crippled men were miraculously healed! They got up from their cots and returned home completely whole in Jesus's name! The residing general superintendent of Malawi, Bishop Kabbalah, confirmed this unprecedented miracle with the Missionary Roy Well.

Pastor David Bounds
Parkersburg, WV

*****

During a crusade in Mzuzu, Malawi, the team and the national church were in the middle of a healing service. As the prayer line started to form, there was a young couple in their mid-twenties that came for prayer. They were well dressed. You could tell that they were not a young couple from the village. They worshipped, they worked the altar, and you could tell they loved and trusted God. I noticed them earlier in the week, and I noticed that they didn't have any children. That was truly odd for their culture. So as the prayer line began to move, people began to get healed and blessed by the power of God that was moving. I looked up, and this couple was standing with tears running down their face. As the team laid hands on their heads and began to pray, a word of prophecy was spoken. Remember, nobody knew about their problem. "Fear not, this night you are healed. You are whole from this day forward. You will be healthy, your children will be healthy, and your husband will be healthy."

They began to shout, worship, and praise God. When the crusade was over and we were getting ready to return back home, we asked the area pastor about the young couple. He began to tell us that they had lived a life of sin before coming to church, and the lady had contracted AIDS. She was afraid of giving her husband AIDS and infecting her child, so they didn't have any children. Two years later we were in Blantyre, Malawi, for a crusade. The same man walked to the altar and asked for prayer for his wife and his unborn child. I realized who he was and began to congratulate him on his child. He clarified that this was his second child that was in need prayer. The first child was perfectly healthy; it was the second child that needed prayer. We began to praise and thank God for what He had done. God healed the second child. There are no shortages on the promises and miracles of God.

The first time that the team was together in Malawi, we were leaving a meeting with the national church leaders. Brother Garlitz told the church leaders that the team wanted to have a crusade for the children as well. They were not too sure about having any kind of church services for the children of Malawi. I remember Brother Garlitz telling them that if they refused to allow a service for the children, then we would refuse to have services for the adults. They reluctantly relented.

I truly believe that was the start of something great among the children of Malawi and for the whole church of Malawi. After that meeting, the team was all loaded up in the van headed back to the hotel. As our driver was driving us down the road and we were all talking about the events of the day, Brother Garlitz made one of his famous statements, "Now, brethren, who's gonna take care of these children and who's gonna go and see these children get filled with the baptism of the Holy Ghost?"

The whole team became quiet. We all looked at each other. I'm sure we were all thinking the same thing: "It's hard enough to do something with children with English-speaking kids at an American

Sunday school, so how can we do this with kids in the middle of Africa who speak a different language?"

A shout rang out from the front of the bus, "Wright, can you do anything with those kids?"

I said, "Yes, sir, I can."

Little did I know that in the next few years, we would see thousands of Malawi children filled with the Holy Ghost, a strong Sunday school department would be formed, and the children today in Malawi would become a big part of the growth of the church in Malawi.

We had about forty children in attendance in our first children's service. The last time we had children's church in Blantyre there were over two thousand children in the service.

The children love to worship, sing, jump, and praise Jesus. To go and see those kids worship and watch God fill them with the Holy Ghost…what a blessing!

One night the team was standing on the platform looking out into the crusade crowd when they noticed that all the children had gold stars or purple or orange or yellow dots on their foreheads. The team asked me, "Wright, what's going on with all the stickers on the children's head?"

I explained that we gave all of the altar workers a card of stickers. When a child received the Holy Ghost, we instructed the workers to put a sticker on their foreheads. At conclusion of the service, we would tell the children with stickers to come to the front of the church. We would get their names and get an accurate count of how many received the Holy Ghost.

As we stood on the platform, the team marveled as they saw all the children with stars on their foreheads. The stars became a trademark. Believe it or not, the starts encouraged the other children to pray and to seek for the Holy Ghost much more because they all wanted a sticker on their forehead.

You could tell when those children received the Holy Ghost because their language changed immediately, and their faces changed.

I remember one night in Blantyre, Malawi, the sun had already gone down that evening. Stars were shining bright, the nationals had finished singing, the dust settled, so it was time for the Word to come forth.

There were two lights that hung off at the end of the platform, and there was one big spotlight that was on the wall of the Bible school that shone over into the crowd. There were about one thousand people on hand that night for the crusade.

The team began to pray that the electricity would stay on for just a few more minutes because the power could go off at any time without any notice or any warning at all. I was called upon to preach that night, and as I began to preach, I began to make my way out into the crowd. As the word went forth and the Holy Ghost began to move, you could just feel that something big was about to happen. In the middle of a sentence, without any notice—*bam!* The lights went out, and the PA went dead!

There I was in the middle of a crowd of people with no lights and no PA. I just kept preaching and shouting the word of God. It seemed like the word just hit the concrete wall and magnified louder so the crowd could hear.

As I looked back at the platform, there stood the whole team with cell phones in their hands, flashlights turned on to give a little bit of light.

As I made my way back up to the platform, the missionary fired up the old generator, and the lights came back on, and the microphone powered up, just in time for the altar call.

That night over 365 Malawi people received the baptism of the Holy Ghost. We all thought, what the adversary meant for evil turned out to be a very special evening for a lot of Malawi people.

With no lights, with no microphone, the Malawi church prayed and praised God even more. Nothing could stop the work that God wanted to do that night.

Rev. Charles Wright
Nashville, IN

*****

When asked to join a Malawi A-Team evangelistic crusade some years ago, I did what many North American ministers do—I checked my calendar and my bank account and weighed my current obligations against my resources of time, energy, and finance. I demurred, frankly, in an attempt to be gracious but to escape yet another commitment in a life that often feels overcrowded.

Thankfully, I have persistent friends, and more pressure was applied. I was told that the experience would transform my ministry. I should confess that I found that claim difficult to embrace. At the time, I had been ministering publicly for three decades, and I figured that, for better or worse, my habits, giftings, weaknesses, and role were all established beyond significant change. Before the first crusade service even began, I learned how wrong I was and how blessed I would be to participate with a team whose apostolic anointing was matched—surpassed even—by Christian character.

Under a thatched roof of a game lodge, I listened transfixed, for hours, as the team leaders honestly and humbly discussed the operation of the Spirit, transcultural ministries, the fallibility of the human vessels that we are, and the great God who condescends to empower the entire enterprise. I will long remember it as one of the most edifying, encouraging, and enlightening conversations of my life. After some days of similar fellowship, team training, and prayer among the North American and European team members, we joined the Malawi national church leaders and our Global Missions family for a time of additional prayer and logistical planning.

At last, our team pulled onto the crusade grounds, where I was struck immediately by two distinct characteristics of the Malawi church—its physical poverty, but its deep, unmistakable joy. Those with greater financial means rode bikes to the meeting place; most walked, in some cases for days. When the worship service began, nothing in my prior experience prepared me for the beauty of that communal singing and dancing—it was music and movement redeemed, to the state of purity and joy before sin and sensuality tainted it and tarnished heaven's glow.

Not all went as planned in the crusade services. It never, ever does in Africa. Power outages, delays, dust, rain, and the beating sun—all contributed to move a fourth-generation North American Pentecostal well beyond his known experience of religious decorum, production values, and expected comforts. But the cooperation and consideration among the national team, the host missionary family, and the visiting team were equal to the task.

And when it came time for the Word to go forth and the Spirit to be made manifest, the Lord demonstrated His sovereignty and power in ways that were undeniable. I personally witnessed people being healed of blindness, deafness, and visible tumors. And even more joyously, during each service, hundreds were filled with the precious gift of the Holy Spirit.

I found myself repenting for the past mistakes of limiting the Spirit of God to the confines of my cultural expectations and tearfully tearing down the idols of retail religion.

I went to Malawi one man and came back another.

Since engaging with the precious people of Malawi, I have never again constrained God by thinking that He needs anything to accomplish His purposes other than His Word, His Spirit, and a willing vessel.

For me, having the privilege of assisting the great church of Malawi in reaching souls has this in common with any other aspect of kingdom work—I have gained more than I have given, and it isn't close. Once a week, or more, my senses will ache for the African dawn, when all the world is awakening, waiting for a syncopated drum to beat out the rhythm of life. But more intently, my soul will long for the liquid black night, when the unmistakable high-pitched keening of the voices of thousands of my brothers and sisters pierces the darkness, and Jesus is glorified under the brilliant stars of the African sky.

Pastor W. Clay Jackson, MD, DipTh
Arlington, TN

*****

Standing in the arena amidst thousands of believers, I could not help but smile as I witnessed the spiritual hunger of the people, because I knew that there would be many miracles that week. Jesus said, "Blessed are they which do hunger and thirst after righteousness, for they shall be filled" (Matt. 5:6).

It never fails—where there is hunger, there will be demonstration. And in Mindanao, that statement was proven in a magnificent way. We learned on the first night of crusade training that Mindanao is referred to as "The Land of Promise" because of the lands fertile soil. People from all over the Philippines have moved into Mindanao because of the fertile land. Every crusade we attend there is an abundance of preparation, including focused prayer, fasting, teaching, and training.

In this particular crusade, we were given the opportunity to meet with the local Bible school students and ministers to teach and to train the concepts of operating in the gift of faith. While sitting outside, protected by a canopy over our heads, heavy rain began to fall, and water literally began to rise on the ground we were sitting on. As each preacher spoke, the water rose higher and higher, threatening the electricity of the speaker system. In the midst of this distraction, God poured out His Spirit that night on these men and women unifying us in mind and in spirit for the coming days of services.

On this same night, members from our team attended a service in a different location where God did an amazing work. The team reported to us that there was a great move of the Holy Ghost in this meeting as over twenty people were filled with His Spirit for the first time. Also, there were several testimonies of healing including a six-year-old crippled boy.

Bro. Andreassan, one of our team members from Norway, was facilitating the altar call when all of a sudden, a young boy was carried up to the platform and sat down in a chair. Bro. Andreassan was informed that this boy had been crippled from his birth and had never walked before. So the team began to pray and lay hands upon him, and suddenly, as shown in the video that was recording this moment, the boy began to feel a tingling in his legs. A moment later that tingling became strength enabling him to stand and walk for the first time in his life. He began walking across the platform, and the crowd went crazy as they understood that this boy had just been miraculously healed. Praise God!

A great gathering had been organized in a large stadium-type auditorium for our main crusade service. Alongside this stadium, a substantial tent was put up for a lady's service that where many ladies were filled with the Holy Ghost. In one day, we held three services at this venue: a youth service, a lady's service, and one main service for all attendees together. It is hard to find the words to adequately describe the excitement and faith that was present in these services. We felt like we could have preached on any truth in the Bible and people would have come to the altar with great expectation.

Several of our team members had the opportunity to speak at the various services, but the greater opportunity came when they witnessed what it is like to see over one thousand two hundred people filled with the Holy Ghost in one given service. I will never forget the image of standing behind Bro. Robinette alongside other members of our team as he prayed the prayer of faith over that congregation of thousands. It was difficult for us to stay focused in prayer and not stand there and watch in amazement as if watching a shooting star or a fireworks display on the Fourth of July.

During this outpouring of God's Spirit, we began to pray for those that needed healing. On foreign soil, prayer for the sick is done much differently than in North America. Healing prayer is very strategic, specific, and intentional, as opposed to a vague, general prayer for God to heal. On foreign soil, people are desperate enough to do whatever is asked of them to receive their healing. That is why we are trained to be very careful what we say to these people, because they will do it. Imagine that being a problem in a North American church. But this is why, in that one service, over five thousand people testified of notable miracles of healing in their bodies. Those who were blind could now see. Those who were deaf could now hear. People with crippled legs and arms were made whole.

No matter how many times I have witnessed God perform the miraculous, I stand in awe amazed by His love and power every time He does it again.

Exposure and faith go hand in hand. Once you are exposed to this power of God, you cannot go back to being average and apathetic.

When you see God heal the sick, you cannot unsee it. This exposure to the miraculous only builds more faith for God to do it again. This is why certain elders among us seem to perpetually walk in the miraculous of God. They have seen it so many times throughout their life that their faith no longer waivers. Exposure to the miraculous leaves no room for unbelief.

The week in Mindanao was concluded with a unique experience, as our team was privileged to preach in over thirty different churches in one day. We split up in groups of two or three, although a few of us went individually. My mission that day took me on a road trip three hours across the island. Although I was tired and fatigued, it was one of the most beautiful trips I have ever seen.

After a long but exciting day ministering throughout the island, the team reconvened that night and gathered that over one hundred souls had received the Holy Ghost in that one day. Altogether, God filled over one thousand five hundred people with the Holy Ghost, sixty-eight people were baptized, and over five thousand people testified of notable miracles of healing in their bodies. This is the results of what happens when a powerful God meets a hungry people; "they shall be filled!" (Matt. 5:6).

> Heal the sick, cleanse the lepers, raise the dead, cast out devils: freely ye have received, freely give... Behold, I send you forth as sheep in the midst of wolves, be ye therefore wise as serpents, and harmless as doves. (Matt. 10:8, 16)

This direction Jesus gave to his disciples includes a promise of demonstration, a warning of persecution, and a word of instruction. Before entering the dimension of demonstration, there must be intentional preparation. Bro. Robinette is very serious about providing an abundance of training and preparation before and during each crusade.

Allow me to share with you what is involved in these training sessions and how God confirmed their importance on the very first night of our Bangladesh crusade when over five thousand people testified of notable healings.

The unique nature of these crusades is that the team consists of men and women from all around the world, most of which have never met before and are experiencing this type of ministry for their first time. It is imperative that we spend ample amount of time teaching, training, and building unity within the group. Outside seeing thousands of people receiving the Holy Ghost, this part of the trip is always my favorite. The ultimate purpose of training is to get everyone on the same page, so that when we enter the crusade grounds, we are a unified army of believers that is both effective and protected. Inevitably we experience opposition and resistance at these crusades, whether it is from witch doctors, governmental oppression, or other forms of spiritual warfare. Therefore, it is vital to be unified and prepared when this attack comes against us.

In the months preceding the crusade, each team member is required to attend conference calls for casting vision and training team members on working with people to receive the Holy Ghost. The team arrives on site two to three days before the first crusade service where we have intensive in-person training and prayer meetings that bring a spiritual unity to the group. It is always amazing watching the new team members step into another dimension of anointing and faith through these training sessions. These two to three days are the most important leading up to the crusade.

From the time we arrive, we do everything together as a team. Breakfast, sightseeing, lunch, prayer meetings, dinner, coffee—it is all done together to build chemistry and unity. This cannot be stressed enough to ensure the effectiveness of the crusade. God can use broken vessels, but He cannot use divided vessels.

Consider a minister that has never laid hands on someone to receive the Holy Ghost, and now they are getting ready to see thousands receive the Holy Ghost. This is the case for most of our first-time team members. Our team is often made up of pastors, worship leaders, teachers, lay ministers, and spouses who have never laid hands on someone and seen a miracle of healing or someone receive the Holy Ghost.

Maybe right now while you are reading this book, you are a minister who has never seen someone receive a miracle while laying hands upon them in prayer. And now you have accepted an invitation to Bangladesh to help see thousands of Muslim and Buddhist people receive the Holy Ghost who have never heard of the Holy Ghost.

You can imagine how valuable it would be to sit down with some elders who have operated in this faith for years and receive personal wisdom and training to be used in this way. This was the setting for our team's first visit to Bangladesh for a Holy Ghost crusade.

On the plane, God gave tongues and interpretation prophesying that He would use this team to see thousands of people receive the Holy Ghost. When God gives tongues and interpretation on a plane, you are sure to arrive with great expectation. During one of our training sessions, Pastor David Meyers taught about three different types of faith that pertained to this crusade: commanding faith, contact faith, and covering faith. The team had decided that the crowd would be too big for us to go around laying hands on everyone in need of healing, so we prayed and believed that God would use us with "commanding faith," which is simply to speak the word of faith commanding healing to take place and sickness to leave. We quickly realized that this was a problem during the altar call of the first night.

We estimated the crowd that first night was at least eight thousand people. The vision for this service was for an outpouring of physical healing. At the conclusion of the preaching, Bro. Nathan Harrod took the pulpit to pray the prayer of faith as the rest of the team stood behind him with uplifted hands. After we all "commanded" healing to take place, about three people claimed their healing. While we are thankful for the three, there were thousands in need of healing in their body. So we prayed again and commanded again that their bodies to be healed. This time two hands went up testifying of their healing. Why were there not more people being healed? Thankfully, Bro. James Corbin, the missionary to Bangladesh, sensed what the problem was. His knowledge of their culture gave him the wisdom that they were not ready for the spoken word of faith, and they needed to make contact with someone.

The people of Bangladesh are "touchy-feely" type of people. It is very ordinary to see two men, platonic friends, holding hands. I found out myself on the last night just how touchy-feely they are when during worship, a group of guys lifted me right off the ground and began tossing me above their heads while they were praising God.

This was one occurrence that was not covered in our crusade training. Bro. Corbin approached the team instructing us, "These people don't understand the word of faith. We need to meet them on their level and go lay hands on them."

There were forty of us and eight thousand of them, but we knew that if the gifts of healing were going to operate, we had to meet the seekers on their level of faith.

Over the next hour, the team laid hands on everyone we could get to, and the spirit of healing began to move like a fire out of control. When the power of God fell, people realized that there was a connection between the healing and the contact made by the laying upon of hands.

As a result, those precious people began desperately reaching for us to make that contact for their healing. Their faith went beyond anything I have ever seen or imagined. Instinctively, I nearly got frustrated as people desperately reached to make contact with me. The people would touch my hand, my arm, and even my shoes, then lay their own hand upon their head for healing. I wanted to correct them that I am not the one they should be reaching for, but I noticed that people were being healed. Immediately the Holy Ghost quickened in me Jesus's response to those healed during his ministry; "Your faith has made you whole."

Their faith did not make sense to me and did not fit my tradition, but yet it was still faith, and God honored that faith just like He honored the faith of the lady who touched the hem of His garment.

This time when we called for a show of hands from those who had been healed, over five thousand people testified of a notable miracle of healing. It was a work of God to have Bro. Meyer teach us about these different kinds of faith that perfectly related to the crusade service the following night.

Never in my life had I considered the concepts of "commanding faith" and "contact faith," nor had I considered the relevance of this in regards to a seeker's level of faith.

Rev. Chris Green
International Evangelist

*****

The Philippines has long been known as the land of revival for many years, and it has been our privilege to take part in many crusades over the years. We have been blessed to partner with our very anointed and capable Filipino leaders and saints, as well as ministries from other countries who have come to join in the harvest of souls in this great country.

Something truly extraordinary happened in October of 2019 when Global Missionary evangelist, Bro. Charles Robinette, and group came for a crusade in Davao, Philippines. The Filipino leaders of the great island of Mindanao prayerfully decided they would call these crusades "Mindanao on Fire!"

The people of Mindanao tend to be cautious when a visitor comes for the first time, as they are very good at reading sincerity and motives. That being said, there was love at first sight with the Robinette team. The excitement was palpable from the start. The schedule of services and the setup of the multiple platforms, both inside and outside, were filled with people. The fire began without the prerequisite "warm-up" and introductory period because the "human blowtorch," Bro. Robinette, lit the fire, and the great team joined in with united focus. The Filipino apostolics took it to another level as every person in the huge crowds were enthralled by the Spirit-saturated air.

When it was all said and done, huge numbers of people were filled with the Holy Ghost for the first time; hundreds and hundreds of miracles of miracles were witnessed. The island of Mindanao is very big, and travel is an enormous challenge; however, most of the pastors were able to attend because the vision of Bro. Robinette was to include every single pastor and leader possible. Bringing more than one thousand pastors together under the circumstances was a daunting task, but with the help of the Lord, it happened!

Mindanao was on *fire*! They took that fire back to their churches, in the coastal remote beachside churches, the mountains, the jungles, even into the predominately Muslim areas, and the fire spread from that one meeting to hundreds of thousands of people. The people of Mindanao can't wait for the return of Bro. Robinette and his very anointed and powerful team!

Rev. Jeff Mallory
President of Hope Village International

*****

During the last two crusades in Bangladesh, God has filled over 12,384 with the gift of the Holy Ghost, and over thirteen thousand three hundred have testified of notable miracles. The testimonies below will surely cause your hearts to leap and faith to rise!

*****

Greater plateaus and plains in the Holy Ghost.

Throughout the last few years, we have watched as the Lord, moment after moment, has been fulfilling His promise of a one-million-soul revival in the nation of Bangladesh. We stand not amazed, for the Lord is the almighty, awesome God, and He moves in His great glory and splendor, but simply grateful!

Years ago, the Lord shewed me a vision of a stone being thrown into a calm body of water. As the stone hit the surface of the calm and even placid water, waves began to proceed outward from where the stone first hit the surface of the water. Immediately, the Lord spoke to me these words: "As this stone hitting the water has caused waves to proceed outward in different directions, so will I use what I am going to do in this nation (Bangladesh) to impact the nations that surround it."

Asia indeed is at the epicenter of the final push in the harvest during these end times, and the greatest move of God's Spirit in Asia and the world is still yet to come. It is even standing at the door and knocking!

Several years ago, after a powerful crusade in which the Lord filled over one thousand three hundred with the gift of the Holy Ghost and healed thousands, I felt strongly impressed of the Lord that we were supposed to conduct crusades every year. The very moment that I was feeling this so incredibly strong for the Lord, the Lord was speaking to Rev. Charles Robinette about Bangladesh. We immediate contacted one another and began to plan the crusade.

After the team from many different parts of the world arrived in Bangladesh, we conducted our first meeting as a team. The Holy Ghost moved in that first meeting and all other meetings following in such a powerful way that it was clear that God not only wanted to reap a harvest for His kingdom in Bangladesh, but He wanted to take the team members to greater plateaus and plains in the Holy Ghost. Individuals with a great hunger for the things of the Lord and to be used by the Lord began to allow Him to flow through them and use them like never before.

During that crusade (2018), 5,382 received the gift of the Holy Ghost and thousands healed in Jesus's name. During the most recent crusade (January 2020), the Lord placed a hunger in a young man's life (crusade team member which was approximately nineteen years old) that he might see God perform a miracle before his own eyes.

A young child was carried in an adult's arms and brought before this young man for prayer. When he looked at the child, he noticed that the child was missing a portion of one of his or her ears and an ear canal as well. He placed both of his hands on the child's head where an ear was and where there was only a portion of an ear and prayed in Jesus's name. When he removed his hands, he noticed that where there was only a portion of an ear, there was now a fully developed ear, and the child could hear perfectly.

Seven thousand received the gift of the Holy Ghost, and over seven thousand were healed in Jesus's name during that crusade!

To God be all the glory and the honor in Jesus's name! The greater plateaus and plains in the Holy Ghost that God is taking the church and nation of Bangladesh to was and is not only for those who were born sons and daughters of the soil but is for those that have bought into and sacrificed much just to come and be a part of God is doing in Bangladesh through the crusade teams as well.

Now the statement of "Take a Missions trip and it will forever change your life" has never been truer. God will change you, your character, and, for many, even your nature and make you into the vessel of honor that you have been called to become and be. In Jesus's name.

Rev. James Corbin
President of the UPC of Bangladesh

*****

Someone of a Catholic background asked the question once, "How do you begin to tell people about Jesus who don't even know Him?"

She continued, "If that person does not own a Bible, how would they know where to find Him?"

Her sincere question was met with a sincere response: First, we believe in being filled with God's Spirit. Second, we believe in the power and demonstration of His Spirit. It was during the Holy Ghost crusades in Bangladesh where we witnessed the supernatural power of God demonstrated through thousands of notable miracles and thousands more receiving the gift of the Holy Ghost.

In 2018, a team of thirty-nine ministers and local pastors stood in the nation of Bangladesh watching as a dark cloud began to roll over the crusade grounds. The atmosphere was charged with anticipation of what God was going to do in that service. It was almost tangible. But due to the superstition in Bangladesh, the approaching storm was thought to be a bad sign that would rain down curses. The people needed a sign from heaven that God was going to rain down His Spirit. As the team started to pray, one of the local pastors (Pastor Peter) began to prophesy. "Our God is the real God," he said. "And it will not rain."

Suddenly, the wind of God began to blow through that place with such divine assurance, and the dark clouds rolled away followed by a sign from heaven. God strategically placed a double rainbow in the sky for all to see that He is the one true and living God—stronger than any other and greater than any storm.

God demonstrated His power that night through many notable miracles. This was one of many miracles, signs, and wonders which God performed during the Bangladesh Crusades.

One night a young girl about eight years old was brought forward to be prayed for. Her mother pointed at the girl's eyes letting us know that she was blind. As I placed my hands over her eyes and began to pray, I noticed her eyes began to move under my thumbs. When I moved my hands away, she looked at her mother and spoke to her in Bangla that she could see. God had just performed a notable miracle by giving that young girl her sight!

Another night during service, a father brought his son to be prayed for. The young boy could not walk, and he had to be held up by his arms. As my husband and another minister began to pray for him, they felt a pop behind his knee, and suddenly the boy began to jump up and down, now able to walk!

Many times, in the Scriptures, we see Jesus performing the miraculous, not just for the sake of miracles but so that the people would believe in Him.

In Bangladesh, we witnessed that very thing. People who would receive a miracle would come back the next night, and God would fill them with His Spirit.

During the 2020 Bangladesh Crusade, thousands of people came forward who needed a miracle from God. One woman in particular had come forward who had previously suffered from a large tumor on her side. Before anyone ever laid their hand on her to pray, that tumor had already disappeared the moment the prayer of faith was released over the people. God healed her of the tumor, and she came back the next night and received the gift of the Holy Ghost! It was during that same service when four girls were standing in amazement as they looked at each other and back at their friend who had just been healed of a tumor behind her ear. The friends inspected her to see where it went. She felt behind her ear and could not find it. Miraculously, the tumor had disappeared when the word of faith was spoken, and the four friends began to rejoice together that she had just been healed of her tumor.

How do we tell people about Jesus who do not know who He is or where to find Him? The power always points to the source (Acts 1:8). What a mighty God we serve! He's a God who desires to manifest His power among us and chooses to use earthly vessels for heavenly purpose.

Rev. Chris and Rev. Amanda Lepper
Bentonville, Arkansas

*****

Miracles! Signs! Wonders! I wholeheartedly believed all of these things to be synonymous with what it meant to be apostolic, as I boarded my flight to Bangladesh. Up to this point, I had heard of the wonder-working power of our God. I had been in services where faith-building accounts of the miraculous were preached. I never doubted that God could and would perform miracles in these days, but I had never seen it for myself. I was hungry for the miraculous, discontent with the norm, unsatisfied with doubt-filled excuses, and craving the supernatural. So as I boarded the plane from Istanbul to Dhaka, my heart was ready to be challenged and thrusted into the often discounted and doubted realm of the miraculous.

I will never forget walking into the crusade team planning meeting. I will never forget walking into this room with full of great men and women of God. These were ministers who had seen miracles and experienced great moves of God, yet they were all hungry and just as desperate as I was for the power of God to be displayed! This hunger united us. It didn't matter what your last name was. It didn't matter what your title was or what position you filled. The only thing that mattered was our mutual hunger. This hunger and desire to be used of God flowed into everything we did as a team. I will never forget the apostolic impartation and radical submission that took place in our team devotions. There was a purity and authenticity to every message we heard. Things happened during these team devotions that I will carry and implement for the rest of my life. The image of Bro. Robinette and Bro. Corbin washing each other's feet in mutual submission is forever ingrained in my mind. The message on being "The Oracle of God" by Missionary Alan Shalm is still ringing in my ears. The tongues and interpretation, the prophetic utterances, and the absolute words from God—it all has been fastened to my mind and left an indelible impact on my future.

Lastly, I will never forget the radical miracles I saw with my own eyes. The precious people of Bangladesh, some who had never even heard the gospel, were hungry for this God we were preaching about. They were so desperate that they would pull and tug on us as they begged for us to pray for them.

Such was the case on the second night of the crusade. I was moving through the crowd, laying hands on as many people as possible (up to this point, I had not personally seen a miracle during the crusade), when this young woman pulled on my sleeve. With tears pouring down her face, she pointed at what seemed to be her baby. It initially wasn't clear what the need was, but as I tried to communicate with the woman, she pointed at the baby's ear—better yet, the area where the ear would normally be. The baby had an ear deformity, which I now know as microtia. There was no ear opening; it was just a ball of flesh. This was no headache prayer request! This wasn't a "my back hurts" request. Though God can heal a headache and though He can immediately take away back pain, there would be no guessing if God had healed this baby's ear. I wouldn't have to ask, "How do you feel?" after praying. No, for this request, there would be visible evidence if God had healed the child. Though my faith was challenged, I prayed with every ounce of faith I had. I didn't scream. I didn't tarry for an hour. I just laid my hands on the ear of that innocent baby and prayed the prayer of faith. After removing my hand,

I almost couldn't believe it—the baby's ear was normal! I didn't have to pray again and again. I didn't have to beg and plead with God. I just followed the teaching of the crusade leaders, prayed the prayer of faith, and God did the miracle.

From that point forward, I saw cataracts disappear, the lame leap, and the mute speak. Going to Bangladesh didn't give me a feeling that miracles were unique to foreign countries, but it taught me that "these signs shall follow them that believe," no matter where we are. This is truly a global harvest!

Rev. Jordan Easter
The Peninsula Pentecostals

*****

Over the years, I have found the crusade ministry to be an invaluable tool in training ministers in how to operate and demonstrate the power gifts. Some of the most beneficial things have been learned in the meetings prior to the crusade services. On the majority of the crusades that I have participated in, we have had times of training on the gifts of the Spirit before we ever stepped foot on the crusade grounds. These were times of prayer and practical teaching on the gift of faith, gifts of healing, and working of miracles. Ministers having the opportunity on how to operate in those giftings and then being able to immediately put into practice what they have learned is what I have seen change so many ministries. Practical teaching on how to pray for someone to receive a miracle and then them having the opportunity to put that into practice solidifies what one has learned. As many have stated over the years, "Many things are caught and not taught."

Because of this, I have tried to take young ministers and other pastors with me to these crusades to "catch" what is imparted in these meetings. My goal has not been to only get these ministers to participate and witness in what God does in these crusade services but to take back to their churches what they have learned and caught in the atmosphere of faith. Every minister that has accompanied me on these crusades have been changed forever!

My assistant pastor, Pastor Rafael, accompanied me on one of the crusades in Bangladesh where he latched on to the teachings and impartation that goes on before the crusade services for the crusade team. It was on the second night of the crusade where I watched as a line formed in front of him and every person that he laid hands on that night was healed. Because he only speaks Spanish, he could not communicate with them directly, so I stood there with a translator who would tell me what they needed prayer for, and I would interpret in Spanish what the need was.

The first was a young boy who was deaf in both ears. As Pastor Rafael laid hands upon him, his deaf ears opened up, and the boy's mother confirmed this miracle had taken place. The next was a man with a large goiter the size of a softball that immediately disappeared when Pastor Rafael placed his hands upon it and prayed in the name of Jesus. After that was a young boy who was blind in one of his eyes that immediately testified receiving his sight when he was prayed for. The impartation he received before the crusade and the activation of faith during the crusade caused him to return to Spain and begin to put into practice what he had learned.

Just a few weeks later he walked into the hospital in the city of Barcelona, where a lady had been in a coma for three days, and spoke the word of faith, and that lady immediately awoke and received the Holy Ghost in her hospital bed. Pastor Rafael has seen hundreds of notable miracles in Spain as a result of the what he caught during that crusade. In another crusade, one of the board members of our organization in Spain accompanied me. He told me later that he had never prayed for someone and seen an instantaneous miracle before in his ministry. It was during the pre-crusade teachings and time of impartation that his faith began to rise and during the crusade that he personally prayed for the blind to see and the deaf to hear and witnessed with his own eyes the miracle working power of our God.

The next week in the church with the pastors in Spain, he put into practice what he had learned and experienced in that crusade and had over seventy testify of miracles and nineteen that received the Holy Ghost with the evidence of speaking in other tongues in his local church. He told me later, "I never thought that God could use me in these areas of faith and working of miracles. What I learned in the training sessions has changed my life and ministry forever."

Many ministers believe that the miraculous can happen, but they aren't sure if it can happen through them, but when put in the atmosphere of the miraculous, they begin to catch what is in the atmosphere. Faith is contagious, and when people hungry for the miraculous are taught what the Word of God says and then can see it demonstrated before their eyes, it becomes more than just a theory. It activates what has been put into them by the Holy Ghost. Once you experience something for yourself, you can never be the same, but it is important to position oneself to be where God is working and imparting.

Every minister that has ever accompanied me on these crusades has not only witnessed with their own eyes thousands of notable miracles, but they have returned to their churches and seen those same miracles happen in their local churches, confirming that what God will do in one country, He will also do in another.

Missionary Nathan Harrod
President of the UPC of Spain

*****

It was my first time in Manaus. It was hot and sticky. The air was thick with humidity. But humidity was not the only thing in the atmosphere. There was a hunger. You could sense it. You could feel it. It was tangible. Our first meeting was at the local Bible college. Sitting in that confined space with a hundred plus Bible college students dressed in white shirts, black bottoms, and black ties, the hunger became a radical expectation. These students didn't just show up for a lecture. They showed up expecting the supernatural. And that is exactly what happened. Bro. Robinette and Bro. Stark began to build the faith that was already there through preaching and exhortation. And then, Bro. Robinette and all the members of the crusade team standing with him stretched their arms over that crowd of students and began to spiritually impart everything the Lord had available. It was incredible. The gifts began to operate. Students were weeping and praying for one another. God was preparing them for the next night.

The next evening, the crusade team and the Bible school students made their way to the Jerusalem center (an outdoor pavilion that sat ten-thousand-plus people built on the banks of the Amazon river). People began to show up by the busloads. Thousands of people filled the pavilion as the worship service began to explode in demonstrative praise. You could feel that God was getting ready to do something incredible. Bro. Robinette came to the pulpit and preached the word of faith. The atmosphere was explosive. Then it happened. Hundreds of people came forward in need of healing. The crusade team, the national ministers, and the Bible school students all lined up across the front of the platform. As Bro. Robinette delivered the prayer of faith, everyone that had lined up across the altar began to move into the sea of people and lay hands on the people. Instantly miracles began to take place. Blind eyes began to open. The deaf began to hear. Tumors disappeared. Crooked legs were made straight. There were literally miracles happening simultaneously in every direction.

The next night, in the same place with the same team, thousands showed up again, and the Lord filled hundreds of people with the gift of the Holy Ghost. It was a weekend I will never forget. It was radical!

Rev. Ventura Azzolini
International Evangelist

*****

Since 2007, AMTC has been the number one training program throughout the UPC-GSN. However, it has only been since around 2015 that we have begun to witness God open unprecedented doors throughout our region. It was when we met Pastor David that God began to give us favor with many unaffiliated pastors throughout our fields. God will allow us to taste what He desires to do until He knows that we can be trusted with the harvest that He has purposed to pour out. He is Lord of the harvest, and He is the one who sends the harvest.

Since 2015, we have witnessed over one thousand one hundred students being trained with the apostolic message. At least 350 have received the baptism of the Holy Ghost, at least 166 have been baptized in Jesus's name, and at least 190 notable miracles have been witnessed. We praise God for all he has done, and we are thankful for the radical sacrifice of numerous North American pastors.

During this end-time harvest that God is pouring out, it is going to look different than anything we might have even experienced. It's going to sound different than anything we might have even expected. Since we have made training a vital part of opening new cities, God has given us pastors who pastor great churches, who never understood the one-God message; however, after a week of training, the majority of them return to their pulpits preaching this apostolic message.

Missionary Nathan Hulsman
Missionary to Switzerland

*****

When I immigrated to Europe, I was drawn to the beautiful message of Jesus Christ and converted to Christianity in July of 1985.

I was a pastor and quickly found a community of African pastors across Europe. It was a blessing to fellowship with people who shared the same difficulties in ministry and life. I was privileged to travel across Europe and teach at several Bible conferences.

While researching the Bible to expand on the topic of my lectures, I discovered more clearly that the same, one and only God who was with Israel in the wilderness, was in the tabernacles, in the temple was in the flesh of Jesus Christ on the cross (John 1:1–3, 14; 2 Cor. 5:19–22).

I spent time sharing this with Ms. Dvora Ganani from the Jewish Agency for Israel, with whom we toured several cities in Belgium and Germany. We invited pastors to come and visit us as well as visit Bible sites for educational tours in Israel.

After hearing me teach, she recommended me to Bishop Robert McFarland of the UPC Biblical Institute—Jerusalem. He began to teach me about essential doctrines such as the oneness of God, baptism of water and of the Spirit in the name of Jesus, etc. I myself was already baptized in a Charismatic church, according to Matthew 28:19–20.

While in Jerusalem in 2015, I received a strong call of God in my heart to return to Europe and start a church in Duisburg, Germany. Bishop Robert McFarland put me in contact with Bishop Charles G. Robinette, who is the general superintendent of the UPC-GSN (United Pentecostal Church—German Speaking Nations)

I was on my way back from Vienna to Jerusalem after conducting a conference at another unaffiliated church led by Pastor Naki Pedro and also a Brazilian church when I met with Bishop Robinette in Duisburg. During our first meeting, I shared with Bishop Robinette the vision that I had which was the same vision that the Lord had given him, a great multicultural and multiorganizational global harvest.

In January 2016, I organized a trip to Duisburg, Germany, to prepare for the opening of the first AMTC (Apostolic Ministry Training Center) in Northern Germany. I had a meeting with Bishop Robinette, who was also the founding president of AMTC, and Rev. Mitch Sayers, the AMTC administrator.

We also met with more than fifteen unaffiliated pastors, including Pastor Pajo Malosa, Pastor Santo do Espirito, Brother Sando Kanda, Pastor Justin, Pastor Nteka Benga, Pastor Mampuya Mbongo, Pastor Naki Mumesso, and leaders of other Christian organizations. Bishop Robinette preached about "Apostolic Demonstration and Power!"

Many pastors repented of their sins and spoke in tongues for the first time. Nine students registered for the Duisburg AMTC campus, and three unaffiliated churches asked to join us as well. (Pastor Naki

Pedro from Vienna; Pastor Pajo Malosa Liége; Brother Christian Kox, who is a German pastor, came with his wife; and many other pastors in Germany were very interested.)

After praying and planning, I returned to Germany from Israel on February 24 to help the team two days before AMTC began. We decided to host AMTC in Brother Sando Kanda's living room. Two days later, we managed to start with nearly fifteen students; most were pastors. Our North American AMTC instructors were Bro. and Sis. Gates from Kansas City, Bro. Hibbert from New York, and Bro. Gratto from Canada.

During our program, Bishop Robinette visited to give a word from the Lord and to show support for our students and instructors. He spoke briefly about Acts 2:37–38. At the same instant, as I was translating for him, I heard an inner voice telling me this now is the opportunity to be baptized in the name of Jesus Christ. I immediately interrupted the bishop and said, "I want to be rebaptized."

He invited others to obey God's word and be rebaptized as well. I was baptized in the name of the Lord Jesus in our Brother Sando Kanda's bathroom by Bishop Robinette with another student and brother, Onya Luciano.

My wife Maria Teresa and my daughters Marie Isabelle Gaziala and Dariela Gaziala were baptized in the name of Jesus Christ the following July.

I felt great joy and peace in keeping God's word and obeying God. I returned to Israel with the strong conviction that I must bring my whole family and come back to Duisburg. I shared this with Bishop Robinette and Bishop McFarland, and they encouraged me to obey God.

After me, the church of Duisburg was able to organize several trainings (AMTC) for many pastors and servants from several cities in Europe. Not only were they trained in apostolic doctrine but also accepted to be rebaptized in the name of Jesus Christ, and they recognized Jesus as the one true God. They no longer baptized in the Trinity formula. Pastor Emmanuel from Dusseldorf was also rebaptized in the name of Jesus.

May 9, Bishop Robinette invited me to Vienna. It was an opportunity for me to strengthen our relationship. I convinced and recommended Pastor Naki Pedro Mumeso and his wife to meet the bishop as well. Since that time, Pastor Pedro Naki Mumeso, his wife, their children, and many of his church members have been able to join the UPC. It was a great experience for me to see many brothers from Syria, Iraq, Iran, and Afghanistan being baptized in the name of the Lord and receiving the gift of the Holy Spirit and speaking in tongues in the Church of Acts in Vienna, Austria.

While I was in Vienna, Bishop Robinette received a call from Pastor Nathan Hulsman, and the bishop asked me if I knew a Congolese pastor Israel Pakasa from Congo who was living in Zurich, Switzerland. I told Bishop, "He is my cousin, but I haven't seen him for a long time."

When I returned to Israel, Pastor Israel Pakasa called me to tell me that he had been contacted by Pastor Nathan Hulsman who was inviting him to the UPC events in Switzerland.

Pastor Israel asked me many questions about the apostolic doctrine. I explained to him and advised him to join our fellowship. He told me, "I know you. I'm going to join and try to convince some pastors that I know to come with me."

Other pastors met with Sister Amber Hackenbruch, missionary to Switzerland. Pastor Israel Pakasa and Pastor Nathan Hulsman— their investments resulted in many unaffiliated ministers being born again.

Pastor Pakasa, his wife, and Sister Amber Hackenbruch in Zurich have so far collaborated with me for the expansion of AMTC in Biel and Couvet where a church was opened in October 2019 as a result. Many Swiss and Africans were born again.

Sunday, 17, I took members of Duisburg from the church where we went to Hagen for fellowship with the church of Pastor Santo Do Espiritu. I translated for Bro. Terry Shock from Louisiana. After the meeting, Pastor Joao Santo was rebaptized in the name of Jesus Christ by Reverend Nathan Hulsman near Hagen. Pastor Santo told me, "I am filled with peace, true peace with the Lord, and joy because, as

I have obeyed the word myself, now I can baptize the people of my church in the name of the Lord Jesus with a free conscience."

During the Elisha Conference in 2016, the message given to us by Bishop Robinette was very clear, "The year 2017 will be double in UPC-GSN." After praying, we immediately started to mobilize students on AMTC campuses. After receiving instructions from Bishop Robinette to open extension campuses from Duisburg to Hagen and Aachen and connect those from Liège to Aachen, I spoke personally with Pastor Joao Santo Do Espiritu from Hagen, Pastor Pajo Malosa from Liège and Brother Gabriel from Aachen to inform them of the vision for the year 2017. All those pastors agreed to work together with me to see this vision become a reality.

In our planning, we prioritized Aachen. We knew the Aachen campus would be the cornerstone of our strategic plan to reach the greatest number of Francophone, Portuguese-speaking, African-born pastors and others in Germany and other countries in Europe.

We had problems finding a permanent campus in Aachen. The doors were closed to us because Pastor Pajo Maloso was not a local pastor. A month before AMTC we decided to directly involve Brother Gabriel to help us get in touch with some pastors locally. We finally found a place to train with Pastor Michel Kaniki. Upon securing a location, I decided to go to Aachen to check everything and meet with the whole team. We were ready to start on Monday, March 6.

I have planned for a class to open in Liège which will be linked to the Aachen campus by video conference built by Reverend Mitch Sayers. This new experience has helped us to attract many students from Liège to register. We had about fifty to sixty students. Pastor Pajo Malosa, a student at Aachen in 2016, accepted to lead a campus in the church where we had five pastors as students. The Liége church can reach between seven hundred to one thousand members, and the Verviers can reach between three hundred to five hundred members. Since 2019, they opened another preaching point in Brussels as well. Bishop Robinette himself, along with many UPCI AMTC instructors, visited Belgium, and in those two visits, God filled nearly three hundred with the Holy Ghost, over sixty were rebaptized in Jesus's name in one service, and nearly three hundred reported notable miracles in those meetings.

The Lord has allowed me to connect many pastors in the cities to follow with AMTC campuses, Köln, Hagen, Duisburg, Aachen, Basel, Zürich, Biel, Neuchâtel, Bienne, Sainte-Croix, Couvet, Liège, Mönchengladbach, Verviers, Munich, Fürth, Nuremberg, Hanover, and so many others.

In February 2020, I have opened contacts to the churches of Romanian communities in the cities of Essen, Dortmund, Gelsenkirchen, and Bochum where we went there with Bishop Robinette to preach there, and in those services, God filled over fifty with the baptism of the Holy Spirit and many testified of miracles.

We are opening AMTC campuses in those cities as well. We are planning a major rebaptism program for these churches as well. We believe that God will allow us to reach many Trinitarian churches across Germany and other countries around to reach the goal of one hundred churches in ten years.

Pastor David Gaziala
Duisburg, Germany

*****

In mid-2017, it seemed good to the Holy Ghost and us (Bishop Khalid Pervais, Bishop Alan J. Shalm, Charles Robinette, and James Stark) to plan a series of meetings in Pakistan. It was Charles Robinette's first trip to Pakistan, and I was very excited to see what God would do through this powerfully anointed vessel there. He arrived in Islamabad, Pakistan, April 10, 2018. The Islamic Republic of Pakistan is a very different world for Westerners. Not only is the culture and language different, but the spiritual atmosphere can also be quite challenging. At the outset of our planning, we were hoping to secure a large outdoor venue for a crusade-type meeting, but the political climate closed several doors, and thus we settled on a multi-meeting format in several areas of the country. Our plan was to base in a guest house in Islamabad and travel to meetings in Sheikhupura, Kharian, and Rawalpindi. We would also be in the headquarters church in Islamabad on Sunday morning. Although this would require us to travel for many hours and not return until well after midnight each night, this was much safer for Westerners than other options. We hired a van and driver for the week. After we arrived in Islamabad, one of the more radical Islamic sects began to foment for political change by organizing a series of violent protests in Islamabad, Lahore, Karachi, and other major cities. We weren't too concerned. Unrest and protest are not uncommon in Pakistan, and we felt that we were there in the will of God. Our first meeting in Sheikhupura would require four to five hours travel on the motorway and put us very close to Lahore. We left Islamabad in the early afternoon, expecting to stop somewhere close to Sheikhupura for some refreshment before the meeting. This was a fairly new church, and they had never had a large meeting like this before. The pastor was excited that we were coming, and we were excited to see what God would do in this new harvest field.

About an hour from our destination, before we left the motorway, we stopped at a very nice (Pakistani standards) rest area that had several fast-food restaurants, including a McDonald's. Brother Shalm, Sister Shalm, Brother Robinette, and I were the only non-Pakistanis in the McDonald's, and in our white shirts and Western-style clothes, we immediately attracted much more attention than we intended to. We placed our orders, and Brother Robinette and I sat in a booth to wait for our food. Very soon, a group of Pakistanis approached us and began taking pictures. We asked them to stop and turned our faces from the cameras. Sister Shalm spoke to them in Urdu and demanded that they stop photographing us. At the same time, a man wearing the bright green turban associated with the radical group that was organizing the national protests came in and took a seat across the dining room from us. He appeared to only have eyes for us Westerners, and he did not appear to be happy that we were there. He videoed us with his phone and just sat and glared at us. When we finished our food, we left for the outdoor ground where the meeting would be held. As we were exiting the motorway, we met a large group of people on motorcycles all going the wrong way on the exit ramp. They surrounded our van and may have wanted us to stop, but our driver kept on going. We arrived at the place where the meeting was to be held, and after Brother Robinette preached, God filled fifty people with the Holy Ghost and about three hundred fifty testified miracles of healing.

Even though we had more than five hours to drive to get home, the pastor had prepared a meal for us, despite Brother Shalm's explicit prior appeal that we really needed to get back on the road. It is almost impossible to decline Pakistani hospitality under these circumstances. It would be a breach of cultural etiquette. We drove to the village where the pastor lived and went into his house. It had been several hours since sundown, but the concrete walls and tin roof did an excellent job of preserving the heat of the day. After almost forty-five minutes, the food was ready, and members of the pastor's family and church members began to serve the guests. It was quite obviously an honor to be present, and the room was filled to more than capacity. While we were eating, Bishop Khalid got a phone call telling him that Islamabad was completely locked down by the protest and that it would be better for us to stay where we were. We had been expecting several busloads of our people from Lahore, but those pastors began to call to say that they were stuck in traffic jams caused by the riots, and they also suggested that we should not attempt to go back to Islamabad that night. Soon all the Pakistanis in the room seemed to be getting news reports that the motorway had been completely shut down, and they all seemed to be very happy that we were going to stay right there until tomorrow or later. I didn't know what I was going to do, but I made up my mind that I wasn't staying in that oven of a house that night. I decided that we needed prayer and opened my phone to find that I had no service in that location. Brother Robinette had service but not much battery, and I asked him to call his wife in Austria and have her call my son, Jimmy, in Columbus to get our ministry team at Calvary praying for us. After about fifteen minutes, I said, "Let's go." We went out to our van, pounded on the side of the van to wake our driver from a deep sleep, and left. We prayed for protection and drove back to Islamabad. We did see some abandoned roadblocks, but we did not encounter one protestor or anyone who attempted to hinder our travel. By the time we got to Islamabad, the sun was coming up, but the roads were clear, and there was no sign of the protests that had paralyzed the city only ten hours earlier.

The next afternoon, we left for Kharion for the annual conference there with Pastor Binyameen. I have been going to Kharion for many years, and it's always a difficult and dangerous trip. The road is called the Grand Trunk Road, and it is clogged with overloaded trucks, speeding busses, motorcycles, and cars. Everybody wants to get "there" ahead of the rest of the traffic. Most of the way is four lanes, but don't think "American Interstate." Accidents are common, and broken-down trucks are even more common. They don't attempt to get off the road. They just put a few branches or some rocks behind them and expect the other traffic to go around them while the drivers and mechanics do major repairs, almost oblivious to the speeding vehicles beside them. There is a large army base at Kharion. It's known as a Cantonment or "CANT." Foreigners are not allowed to pass through or venture onto a CANT. It says so in big bold letters on my visa. In order to get to the church, we have to navigate around the CANT, which adds time to the already lengthy trip.

Pastor Binyameen always organizes the conference well and knows that the important elements of a harvest meeting are worship and the Word. He does not allow the service to be lengthy or drawn out. He introduces the speaker in good time and always has a good crowd of people who need the Holy Ghost. The conference is held on a lot behind the church, and there were about six hundred fifty people in attendance that evening. After Brother Robinette preached, God filled about fifty people with the Holy Ghost, and about one hundred fifty people testified to miracles of healing. Pastor Binyameen understood that we had three to four hours to drive, and he allowed us to go directly from the platform to our van to begin our trip home. About an hour up the road, we stopped at an all-night KFC, and, "on the strength of that meal," we made an uneventful trip back to our guesthouse in Islamabad.

On Sunday morning, at the R. G. Cook Memorial Building in Islamabad where Bishop Khalid is the pastor, more than four hundred fifty people crowded into the second-floor sanctuary. At the close of that service, God filled seven people with the Holy Ghost. That evening, we traveled about an hour to the city of Rawalpindi. This is the city where Brother Billy Cole preached an outdoor meeting in 1996. In that meeting, a crowd of approximately eighty thousand people gathered, and God filled about three thousand of them with the Holy Ghost. Our meeting was in a convention hall on the same ground where Brother Cole had preached in the open-air meeting. Nearly a thousand people gathered that evening, and after Brother Robinette preached the Word, God filled about one hundred twenty people with the Holy Ghost, and about four hundred testified to miracles of healing. By Monday evening, we were on our way to the airport to head west. Brother Robinette went back home to Austria, and I was on my way to Ohio. The next day, Brother and Sister Shalm returned to Malaysia to continue their missionary ministry from there.

Bishop Jim Stark
UPCI District Superintendent Ohio

*****

The Alaska-Yukon District is a very unique district in the fact that our churches are extremely remote, and most of the churches are smaller churches and very rarely are able to have a guest evangelist for a revival. As the NAM director, I had a desire to help the smaller churches with a Holy Ghost rally at as many places as we could get possibly visit. As I began to pray and seek God about this, I very strongly felt to call Bro. Robinette about coming to be the speaker. As soon as he heard the idea, he was all in, and we booked a date for him to be in our district for eight days. I distinctly remember talking with him about the schedule and how many days he would like to preach and how many days he would like to have off. He adamantly told me, "I want to preach every night and multiple times on Sunday." So in eight days we saw an unprecedented 112 filled with Holy Ghost, 27 baptized, 143 miracles of healing in ten services in eight days. It was simply miraculous and greatly impacted many churches in our district.

I remember him preaching for a church in Anchorage for a pastor who had never been in an international crusade. By the end of service, they had several HG-filled and miracles, and Bro. Robinette had also raised a $5,000.00 offering for the local pastor to go to the crusade in Bangladesh. I remember thinking, here is a missionary coming to a church, and instead of him raising an offering for his needs, he raised a substantial offering for the local pastor. What an amazing kingdom-minded action that forever changed a local pastor.

Our friendship was God-ordained from the beginning. It was at a conference that we were both speaking at that God connected us in a very special way. Since that time till now, I have learned to value and appreciate the incredible anointing and gifting that God has placed upon Charles Robinette, and only eternity will tell the multitude of lives that have been impacted all over the earth because of his truly apostolic ministry.

Pastor Jim Blackshear
Anchorage, Alaska

*****

We pastored the Church of Acts in Vienna, Austria, from 2006–2017. We witnessed many notable miracles during those eleven years that were catalyst for unprecedented harvest in the nation of Austria and beyond.

During one of our weekly prayer meetings at the Church of Acts, a Muslim couple walked into the church. They were both dressed in traditional Muslim attire. They stood along the back wall of the sanctuary and watched us pray for a lengthy period of time. Toward the end of the prayer meeting, I walked to the back of the sanctuary and asked the couple, "What brings a Muslim couple to a Pentecostal church during a prayer meeting?"

The man responded, "If we had any other options, we wouldn't be here."

This of course made me laugh out loud. I said, "Well, you're here. What can we do for you?"

The man proceeded to tell me of the pain and suffering they had experienced over the last ten years that I'll try to summarize below.

The Muslim couple was medically unable to conceive and bear a child. They went through ten years of medical treatments at a great, personal financial expense in order to conceive a child and nothing worked. The morning before they visited our church, their personal physician met with them and told them that there was absolutely nothing left to do medically. The Muslim man took his wife home and went to work. While working alongside a Catholic man that evening, the Catholic man realized the Muslim man's countenance was different and asked him what the problem was. The Muslim man told him they had reached the end of all their medical options, and they would never be able to conceive a child. The Catholic man turned off the machine they were working on together and said to the Muslim man, "I'm Catholic, so there is nothing I can do for you. But if you can find a Pentecostal church, the God of the Pentecostals can do things that no other God can do." They googled "Pentecostal churches in Vienna" and found the Church of Acts.

The Muslim man looked at me and asked me the question, "Do you think that the God of the Pentecostals would be willing to heal a Muslim man and woman so they could conceive a child?"

I told him, "Absolutely!"

We called the elders together at the back of the sanctuary. We told the Muslim couple that we would lay hands on the Muslim man, and he would lay his hands on his wife.

We prayed for God to do an immediate miracle and that they would conceive a child. Nothing dynamic happened. The Muslim couple wept as we prayed, but their emotional response was born out of their pain at being unable to conceive and out of the kindness that these Christians from the Church of Acts were demonstrating toward their family. They left the church that evening, and we did not see them again for about nine months.

On a Sunday morning, about nine months later, the Muslim man came dramatically into the church and came all the way to the edge of the platform and said to me, "Pastor, do you remember me?"

I said, "Yes, sir," and I called him by his name.

He said, "You prayed for us to conceive a child, and I've just come from the hospital where my wife just gave birth to twins!"

I said, "Praise God, why didn't you come back after you conceived so that we could have celebrated with you what God has done?"

He said to me, "God did not do this. It is only a coincidence that we conceived after you prayed."

I said, "Okay, then why are you here now?"

He said, "Our babies are on life support. The doctors said they will not make it through the night. They are not breathing on their own and are very weak. Do you think that the God of the Pentecostals would heal two Muslim children?"

I said, "Absolutely! But not unless you confess that Jesus Christ is God!"

The Muslim man fell on his knees and began to weep at the altar calling out the name of Jesus. We called for the elders of the church, and we prayed for the Muslim man and his newborn children. Nothing dynamic happened. The Muslim man stood up, thanked me, and returned to the hospital.

Later than evening, I received a phone call from the Muslim man. He said, "Pastor, do you recognize my voice?"

I said, "Yes, sir," and I called him by his name again.

He was weeping and very emotional. He said, "Pastor, guess what *our* God has done? When I returned to the hospital, my children were off life support and breathing on their own! The doctors are in shock! Jesus has healed our babies! Can we bring them to the church next Sunday so they can be dedicated to the Lord Jesus Christ?"

I said, "Absolutely!"

The next Sunday, the Muslim man and woman returned to the Church of Acts in Vienna, Austria, with their two newborn babies.

During the baby dedication, the Holy Ghost fell upon that family! The Muslim man began to shake uncontrollably. We took the babies out of their arms. The Muslim woman reached over to brace her husband. When she touched him, the Holy Ghost fell upon her, and she began to tremble as well! Both of them were filled with the Holy Ghost, speaking with other tongues in the middle of their babies' dedication service. They were both baptized that same day in the only saving name of Jesus! That was the beginning of the great Muslim revival and harvest in the nation of Austria.

Not too long after that miracle, we were contacted by a family member of a devout Muslim who was studying at the university in Vienna. During Ramadan, this Muslim brother had a dream. In the dream he saw Jesus Christ sitting upon the throne in heaven. He began to search for people in Vienna who believed that Jesus Christ was God manifested in the flesh.

To make a long testimony a bit shorter, this Muslim brother came to our church on a Sunday morning right before Apostolic Ministry Training Center (UPC-GSN Bible School) began its next semester. He was anxious to begin studying the Word of God, but he did not yet have the Holy Ghost, and he was not yet baptized in Jesus's name (which were both mandatory requirements before applying to AMTC). The Lord spoke to me and told me to allow the Muslim brother to join AMTC even though it violated the established policy. I decided to take it a step further than God required and told the Muslim brother that he could join AMTC, but he had to be filled with the Holy Ghost and baptized in Jesus's name before the first week of training ended or he was out.

Many ministers including Missionary Radovan Hajduk and Missionary Nathan Hulsman taught during that semester of AMTC in Vienna. Together their doctrinal investment bore fruit during one of our evening classes. During the instruction, the Muslim brother jumped to his feet and began to shout the name of Jesus. Moments later he was speaking with other tongues. Six days later, on Sunday morning, the full revelation of the mighty God in Christ overtook that Muslim man. He was baptized in Jesus's name that morning and came out of the water speaking with other tongues.

The Muslim man graduated from AMTC, and while he was faithful to the Lord, God used him in a mighty way. He assisted me, and we launched a Farsi-speaking preaching point in Vienna, Austria, that resulted in over 101 Muslims being filled with the Holy Ghost and 159 Muslims being baptized in Jesus's name in a very short period of time. When we left Vienna in December 2017, the Farsi preaching point was thriving and continued to bear fruit on a weekly basis.

In the midst of God's Muslim harvest in Vienna, Austria, a film director visited our service on a Sunday morning. He had been tasked with creating a documentary which would be viewed at the European film festivals and was supposed to focus on the humanitarian crisis due to the mass Muslim migration in Europe. During our service, he saw something he did not expect. He witnessed Muslims worshipping Jesus Christ alongside twenty-one cultures of Christians. He witnessed Muslims repenting of their sins, being filled with the Holy Ghost, and being baptized in Jesus's name. After one service, he came to me and said, "I've realized that there is no Muslim crisis where there is the power of the Holy Ghost! Would you mind if I use your church and do a documentary about how Pentecost is changing the lives of Muslims?" After lengthy negotiations, we agreed, and the camera crew arrived on a Sunday morning. It was lights, cameras, and Holy Ghost actions! Many Muslims were filled with the Holy Ghost that day and baptized in Jesus's name. They interviewed two of the Afghanistan Muslims, Bro. Nabi and Bro. Dawood, who we won to the Lord in the beginning of the Farsi church. The night that Bro. Nabi and Bro. Dawood received the Holy Ghost and were baptized in Jesus's name, they were beaten for their faith when they returned to the refugee camp, and told that if they returned to the Church of Acts, they would be killed. They returned the very next service and brought even more Muslims with them who wound up receiving the Word of God with gladness and were also born again. I don't remember how many people those two precious Afghanistan Muslim brothers brought to the Lord, but I know this: God will not forget the price they paid for propagating the gospel nor the Muslim souls that received their testimonies with joy!

Rev. Charles G. Robinette
UPCI Missionary to Germany, Switzerland,
Liechtenstein, and Austria

*****

Pastor Paul Mooney shared this testimony following a deputation service at Calvary Tabernacle in Indianapolis, Indiana, from a man who was watching the service live on the internet:

There's a reason I said the Spirit of the Lord works wherever you are at, as long as you are willing. Throughout the whole service I felt a tug on me. Toward the end of the service, my legs and arms and hands started to shake. The same as they did the night I first went to the altar and the same as they did the night I got baptized. I sat on this couch shaking with an uncontrollable tremble through my body. I felt something with me. Something in me! I raised my hands, and I said, "God, I'm sorry. God, I love you, and I want to be with you and walk with you!" At that time, my jaw started trembling, and my tongue started moving, and I just jumped up ripped my headphones from my ears and started walking around this apartment speaking things I've never said before. It went on for minutes. When I sat down again, the pain I've had in my neck for three days was gone, and I felt renewed. Felt joyous and happy and peaceful.

*****

Pastor Hal Modglin shared this testimony with our Malawi Crusade team after we left Africa:

Praise report! Wanted to let everyone know the results of what God has done for me through your prayers on our missions' trip. As many of you remember, Brother Robinette had our team pray for me while in South Africa. From all indications, it looked like I had prostate cancer. However, last week I went to M. D. Anderson, and when my blood work came back, it had dropped in half. An MRI was done, which came back clear. I am thanking God for this healing and thanking the team for their prayers. We serve an awesome God!

*****

Pastor Dwaine Chapdelaine shared this testimony with us following our deputation service at Cornerstone Church in Kalamazoo, MI:

A lady in my church just called me. She was the woman who brought the little baby up to be prayed for. The baby was medically diagnosed with a very serious issue: her head was enlarged, and she needed a helmet on her head. We prayed over that baby on Sunday, and she went to the doctor today, and the doctors can't understand what has happened, but the baby's head returned to its normal size that it's supposed to be at. The baby is completely healed! The grandmother just called me as well, weeping and shouting praise to God!

*****

Bro. Andrew Miller shared this testimony with me after a deputation service:

The Sunday after you were here, we received a few testimonies of the miracles of God in peoples' lives as a result to prayer. One sister who we prayed for the Sunday you were here had been suffering from severe migraine-type headaches and had been diagnosed with some type of neurological disorder. At times half of her face would become somewhat paralyzed. But the next Sunday she testified that she was better and hadn't felt any pain or experienced any type of paralysis all week. Also, that next day I went to the doctor to have my checkup and receive results from some previous exams and labs. I'm happy to report that God took care of me, because without having to take any medication or anything, only prayer, the doctor's report was great. He told me that as we compared the preliminary exams to the secondary exams, that things had definitely changed. The lump that was by my neck is completely gone. My liver panel came back showing my liver is in excellent condition. No problems there. Plus my blood pressure showed a perfect 120/80. I was given a clean slate. All's well, thank God!

*****

The following reports are from testimonies that occurred while we were on deputation in the United States. The reports were taken from our missionary update letters.

- We have had several healings since our service together. I have been so excited about all the miracles occurring lately. One sister reported being healed of lung cancer. X-rays were taken the day of her scheduled biopsy, and the tumors and signs of cancerous growths on her lungs were no longer anywhere to be found. The doctors did not even do the biopsy because there was no longer anything to biopsy! Praise God!

- Another report just two weeks ago was from a sister who had a large cyst growing over the last three years on the back of her neck. She is an older saint in our church. She described that it had grown to the size of an egg, and she could feel it spreading, literally around her neck. She said it almost felt like it was spreading to strangle her. At Monday night prayer meeting, she told the church how she didn't tell even her daughter about the cyst…just was not inclined to. She is a nurse, and she just gave it to God. When it started to spread around the sides of her neck, she became a little more concerned, and when you were at our church preaching and told people who wanted a healing to come up and receive it, she felt the unction to go to the altar for prayer. No one had prayed over her about her cyst because she had not, up until that point, told anyone. She was even wearing clothes that would purposefully hide the egg-sized cyst. After you prayed over her, she noticed in the ensuing days that the cyst was shrinking. Something started to ooze out of it, and each day she would check it and wipe the oozing fluid off. When she reported the miracle to everyone two weeks ago, she said that it was now completely gone. No trace of it! Hallelujah to the Lamb! Love in Jesus.

- I was hearing impaired before the service. When I woke up the next morning, I could hear the birds chirping, the water running, and the wind blowing! All praise to God who still causes the deaf to hear!

- Before service one night, our baby had an allergic reaction. We called the hospital, and they strongly encouraged us to bring our child in immediately. We decided to bring him to the house of the Lord instead. We brought our baby to the front to be prayed for. He had red marks all over his face, and we told you the hospital wants us to bring our baby in now, but we know God can do it Himself. When you began to pray over our baby and before we returned to our seats, the fever was gone, and the red marks disappeared! Mighty God!

- I had severe asthma before the service. I could not go one day without using my inhaler at least three times daily. I could not worship the way I wanted to because I would begin to lose my breath. But while you were preaching last night, I began to hear the Lord tell me, if I would worship Him, He would heal me! I started running and praising God with all my might. When I left the service that night, I had not felt that strong in years! When the week ended, I still had not used or needed my inhaler one time! God is still able to do anything!

- I have never been one to believe in miracles, but now God has changed all of that for me! I needed surgery on my leg. I had a hip replacement that didn't go right. A doctor made one leg longer than the other. For over one year, I lived in so much pain. I could not stand straight, and I was constantly on pain pills. The doctor was going to do surgery again and try to stretch my muscle. My pastor Bro. Lewis had been preaching about faith when Bro. Robinette came and preached about miracles. They prayed for me, and God opened my eyes and showed me that He can do anything if we will just believe. God made my leg grow instantly without surgery! God took all my pain away instantly! My doctor was so amazed! After the x-ray, he did not know what to say. Not only has my leg grown, but I have begun to grow taller, which they said was not possible. All the glory goes to the Lord Jesus Christ!

*****

Pastor Soto called me on the phone and said, "Someone wants to say hello to you. Do you remember the guy who had dreadlocks and piercing at the youth rally? You would never recognize him now!"

The man got on the phone and said, "I must tell you my testimony. I was being treated at the Mayo Clinic for seven years. I have had multiple surgeries, been through radiation treatments, and after all that, they told me the cancer was still there. But the night when I got the Holy Ghost, something happened to me. I went back to an apostolic church, got baptized in Jesus's name, and the next week I went back to the Mayo Clinic for my regular checkup. They could find not one trace of cancer or any tumors in my body! Four months later, there is still no sign of cancer!"

Pastor Aaron Soto
Appleton, WI

*****

We had long prayed and believed in the German-Speaking Nations that God would send us a multigenerational, multilingual, and multicultural revival. The Lord did just that when a door opened with the Farsi- and Arabic-speaking communities of Vienna in May 2016.

Much prayer had gone into our first service in the Farsi language, and none of us were quite sure what to expect. As we were praying and preparing at the church before the service, we looked out the window and saw a beautiful sight that I will never forget: a large group of precious Middle Eastern people exiting the tram and walking down the street to our church.

All of these people had been raised Muslim. Some of them had come to Europe during the refugee crisis a few months prior. Some came to the church service that night at the risk of their own physical safety. God showed up in a beautiful way and again the next day as the group came back for our Sunday service. By the end of that weekend, ten people had been baptized and Holy Ghost-filled, and an amazing revival began.

There are so many beautiful stories from this season that they could fill the pages of their own book. Many of those that were won during this time had no prior experience with Christianity or church. Bro. Robinette and other leaders in the church taught Bible studies to the group with Farsi translation each week. Bro. and Sis. Terry Shock, Bro. and Sis. Chris Green, and Bro. and Sis. Nathan Hulsman came to do a special time of teaching with them and invested many hours talking with individuals from the group and teaching them foundational doctrine.

Many were enrolled in AMTC, the Bible school of the GSN. As they grew in understanding, they began inviting more and more people to the meetings, and God began filling more and more with His Spirit.

I will never forget the young Iranian family that immigrated to Austria with a newborn baby. Their first service, they wept on Bro. Robinette's shoulder as the presence of God moved upon them. Both of them were baptized and received the Holy Ghost, and they dedicated their precious baby to the Lord soon after. I will never forget the first woman who began attending Farsi services. She received the Holy Ghost during a ladies' prayer meeting. We did not have a translator for her that day, and she spoke no English and only a few words of German. But we serve a God who speaks all languages, and as we began to pray, tears flowed down her face, and she began to speak with other tongues.

I will never forget the look on their faces the day that Bishop James Stark was with us and told the group of an Iranian man at his church in Ohio that wanted them to know he was praying for them. The thought of someone from their own culture who had also met Jesus and was thinking of them from across the ocean deeply touched them. Several who had not yet surrendered to God received the Holy Ghost that weekend.

I will never forget the weekend of our Elisha Conference in 2016, when Bro. Raymond Woodward preached and one of my precious friends was baptized and received the Holy Ghost! She was a student at the university and was always a bit reserved during our church services. The day she made the decision to get baptized, she came out of the water shouting at the top of her lungs, speaking in tongues and rejoicing!

At the one-year anniversary of our first Farsi service, Bro. Landon Gore preached, and we heard testimonies from some of the members of what God had done in their lives. We wept as they told stories of how God ordered their steps to our church, how He was revealing Himself to them, and of the sacrifices they made and the blessings they received in their conversion.

"I went to another church in Vienna, and they yelled at me and told me to get out. I thought, Christianity is no different than Islam. But I prayed that God would show Himself alive to me if He was really God. Within twenty-four hours, a miracle happened in my life. And then He led me to this church," said one member.

"I was scared to convert from Islam to Christianity for fear of losing my traditions and my family. But when I came out of the waters of baptism, all fear lifted from me. And now God has given me a new family,' said another.

God is the God of *all* peoples. We are in the last days, and He is truly pouring out His spirit on all flesh. As time went on, some of those in the group carried their experience with Jesus with them to other countries and some back to their home nations.

I am thankful for the unique window of time the Lord gave us to share Him with these precious people, and that He allowed us to witness firsthand this incredible revival. Since that revival began, 159 Muslim people were baptized in Jesus's name, and 101 filled with the Holy Ghost in Vienna, and even more across our region. All flesh. He's still moving!

Rev. Whitney Bateman
UPCI Associate Missionary

*****

Praise the Lord! I'm writing this because the Lord changed my life, and I want my testimony to be a blessing to the work of the Lord! There is nothing more beautiful than knowing Jesus Christ, knowing the truth, being baptized in Jesus's name, being filled with the holy spirit, and being free from darkness forever.

I was a lonely guy who was surrounded by *lots of religious people* and ritualistic cults. Our family was "Shayah Islam," which is a part of Islamic religion. Shayah Islam is a large part of the religion and politics in the nation of Iran. It was so important for each individual in Iran to follow the protocol of this religion.

I was sad every day. I felt empty because I was listening to my aunt and also my family which were trying to control my life. One day, after five years of the faith, I was so tired of doing the Islamic rituals, and I asked my father, "Why doesn't God answer my prayer?"

My father looked at me and said, "Maybe you are doing something wrong, my son. I don't know, but never give up seeking God. I'm sure He will answer you."

I was encouraged by what my father told me, but when I returned to my room, darkness and sadness attacked me again. I was eighteen years old, and I became depressed because God never answered my prayers. I kept wondering about what was wrong with me. How could a person pray five years, do all the Islamic rituals, and still get nothing from God? I felt like my life was over. I had lots of problems. I even received a warning from the Islamic Revolutionary Guard, and they stopped me from studying in university. They blocked my life completely. They even threatened to put me in prison.

I could hear and feel the devil whispering in my ears, "Hey, Reza, it's the end!" I started looking online for a way to leave Iran. I searched until early in the morning. I was so tired and without energy. I started to cry and shouted to God, "Help me, I need you in my life. Where are you? I prayed to you for five years, but you didn't answer me!"

I was tired. I lifted my head up, and I wanted to log out of my Facebook page, and I saw a picture of Jesus Christ that one of my Facebook friend's posted. On the top of this picture was a verse of the Bible that said in Persian: Luke 11:9–11, "So I say to you: Ask and it will be given to you; seek and you will find; knock and the door will be opened to you. For everyone who asks receives; the one who seeks finds; and to the one who knocks, the door will be opened."

I prayed, "I say your name, Jesus. Change my life or I will end my life tomorrow."

I went to the bed, and I fell asleep. I saw the Lord in my dream. I did the same Islamic rituals in my dream. Jesus came near me and put His hand on my shoulder and said, "What are you doing, my son?"

I looked at Him, and I was amazed by His beauty and glory. I said, "Lord, I'm doing my prayer for help."

Jesus said, "Come with me, Alex. Your name will be Alex. I will show you the light and the way. *I am the way!*"

He said that If I followed Him, He would give me a peace and joy. Then He said to me, "I will introduce you to my best friends. Listen to them and they will help you."

Then in my dream, seven years before I ever met Him, seven years before I ever saw Him, Jesus showed me Pastor Robinette. After I woke up, I had a wonderful feeling for two weeks! Miraculously, all the doors opened to me, and I left Iran! The Lord sent me to Austria. I found the Church of Acts, I saw Pastor Robinette for the first time, I got baptized in Jesus's name, and I was filled with the Holy Ghost. I was amazed! I said, "How can it be?"

I saw Bro. Robinette seven years earlier in my dreams! Pastor Robinette was a best friend of the Lord! Glory to the name of Lord Jesus Christ.

I found peace for living! I found the truth! I asked Jesus, and He showed Himself to me. I thought there was no God, but Jesus showed Himself to me. Jesus showed me that He existed, and He will work in our life when we ask Him to. God bless you all. I pray for a wonderful life for you all and wish the Lord always protects you in every step in your life.

Bro. Reza (Alex) Namdari
Muslim Convert

*****

It amazes me to this day that just about four years ago, I was able to bear witness to an unprecedented revival among the Farsi-speaking population in Austria. In almost every service, we were baptizing multiple, former practicing Muslims, in Jesus's name. And every week, more and more Muslims came to have their own life-changing experience.

Within the first year, we had over one hundred Farsi-speaking brothers and sisters baptized in Jesus's name and almost as many filled with the Holy Ghost. It was amazing to see how hungry these new Christians were to learn about the Lord Jesus.

I love the way God can use a difficult and challenging situation as a way to bring people to the revelation of one God in Christ Jesus. These were people who in their home country had very little to no access to the gospel. For many of them, becoming refugees in Austria was the only opportunity to learn about Jesus and the love and freedom the Word of God can bring. Not only were the lives of our new brothers and sisters changed, but the experience also had a profound impact on all those that witnessed what the Lord was doing in Austria.

Bro. Jordan Dunning
UPCI AIM Worker

*****

I arrived in Austria in 1994. A year later I joined a trinitarian church, where I got baptized in the name of the Father, and of the Son, and of the Holy Spirit in 2006. My family and I moved to London in 2008. I had my own plans to be involved in politics, but I experienced a complete turnaround of my own plans.

The Word of God says in Isaiah 55:8, "For my thoughts are not your thoughts, neither are your ways my ways. saith the Lord."

In 2010, I was called by the Lord to serve Him in the pastoral ministry. It was a hard time for my family to accept God's decision. My pastor at the time got a revelation of my calling, and after some time in prayer, God confirmed the decision to us. And we accepted

God's decision. God then later revealed to my wife that I would not be ordained in London. Three years later God spoke to us clearly that we had to go back to Vienna for His work. Our stay in London was our preparation for the ministry. And in 2015, we returned to Vienna. While my family was on holiday in Vienna, I started looking for a church to worship God during our holiday. During that period, my wife found and picked up a Church of Acts leaflet on the seat of a number 71 tram. When she came home, she showed me the leaflet. After reading it, the spirit of the Lord led my wife and me to visit the following Sunday. Surprisingly, we knew a sister at the church who worshipped at the COA, and she introduced us to Pastor Charles Robinette. It was the first time we met him. We were warmly welcomed by him. I still remember the topic of the sermon which was about the one name of Jesus. After the service, he invited us to his office, and we talked to him about the plan of God to open a French church in the city of Vienna.

Without hesitation, he made himself available to us in any way that he could. In the meeting, he proposed for me to join the one of the UPCGSN training initiatives, Purpose Institute. It was beginning the following week. I joined Purpose Institute, and my wife and I decided to make the COA our home church.

A few days before my family went back to London, the Lord spoke to my wife in a dream that I should baptize our daughters in Jesus's name, but they had to travel before the next Sunday service, so I decided to baptize them in the Danube before they left.

While attending the Church of Acts, I heard several teachings about the oneness of God and baptism in Jesus's name. All those teachings made me understand that I needed to be rebaptized because as I said earlier, I was baptized before in the name of the Father, and of the Son, and of the Holy Spirit.

During COA services, the Holy Spirit kept reminding me that I have to obey the word of God by getting baptized in Jesus's name. The enemy was always trying to persuade me that I was already baptized and that there was no point. Every time I decided to get baptized, I heard a voice telling me, "Everyone knows you as a pastor. Are you not ashamed to be baptized?"

I backtracked on my decision each time. It happened to me multiple times. What I learned is the Lord Jesus is so patient. In our life, there is always one day where the Holy Spirit moves into someone's life and decides to do whatever He wants; there is no resistance.

One Wednesday service changed my life! While Pastor Robinette was preaching about baptism in the name of Jesus, I felt in my heart that it was my day, and the Holy Spirit spoke clearly to me that I couldn't miss that opportunity, and my entire body was shaking from the inside out. The Holy Spirit reminded me that I was baptized in the Trinitarian formula. After the service, I spoke to Pastor Robinette what I experienced during the service, and I told him that I had to be rebaptized. And he told me, "If you don't mind, can we do it on Sunday?"

I couldn't wait! I replied, "No today is today."

It sounded like in Acts 8:36, the story of the Ethiopian eunuch and Philip: "And as they went on their way, they came unto a certain water: and the eunuch said, See, here is water; what doth hinder me to be baptized?"

Faith that saves is inseparable from obedience to the word of God. And obedience is better than sacrifice, says the Lord. I couldn't care what people may think of me. Pastor Robinette rebaptized me in the only one saving name of Jesus. And when I came out the water, the Holy Spirit moved in a mighty way that I cannot explain even today. We serve an amazing God who is able to do whatever He wants in our lives.

No one is capable to stop the blowing wind of the Holy Ghost. After the baptism, I called my wife who was in London. I explained to her what the Lord had done in my life, and since then I began to teach her what I received. She also was touched by the Word of God and decided that once she was in Vienna at the COA, she will also get rebaptized, which she did. My whole family is now baptized in Jesus's name. Praise the Lord.

We are so thankful to the Lord Almighty. We are also thankful for the man He connected us to, Pastor Robinette, and his family who have a major impact in our lives in general, especially in my ministry. He's a man with a big heart, a carer for souls, and a mentor. He's a humble man of God. I sincerely thank you for all your love, encouragement, and support toward my family. Thank you also for implementing the very first stone for ADiPE Church.

I would also like to thank Pastor and Sr. Pace, all the saints of COA, and lastly, thanks to UPC-GSN General Board for everything they're doing for the ADiPE Church in Vienna, Austria. May the Lord bless you, Bishop Robinette.

Pastor Rachedie Mubobo
Vienna, Austria

*****

Since the beginning of our ministry in 1987 in Soyo, Angola, as pastor, we baptized in the Trinitarian formula (Acts 2: 38).

And we also spoke in tongues, but we still taught the doctrine of the Trinity. We arrived in Austria in 2000, and in October 2007, we had planted a church in Vienna: Mission New Covenant of Christ; officially recognized in 2015.

It was when we returned from our trip to Israel that we made contact with Bishop Charles G. Robinette and were able to make an appointment. This was a divine connection. We met in March of 2016.

Our daughter Gabriela served on the COA worship team; my wife and I had the privilege of serving as teachers of the Word in COA alongside Bishop and Sis. Robinette, who at that time were missionary pastor and general superintendent of UPC-GSN. It was the time provided by God to also experience a seasonal transition in our ministry. As the pastor of the New Covenant Mission Church of Christ, we were looking for another location for our services. As we already knew Pastor Robinette, we told him that we wanted to meet in their building, and doing so would make it easier for him to give seminars on biblical teachings to our church. With an open heart, he accepted me and offered for us to occupy their facility Sundays at 4:00 p.m. His proposal was welcomed to me.

Over time, in a common agreement, we decided instead of the two churches meeting in the same building at different times, it would be better to have only one church. We merged the two congregations into one 11:00 a.m. service.

There is one common denominator between the doctrine of the Trinity and the doctrine of oneness: Jesus Christ. But there is a central point of divergence. This disagreement made me uncomfortable on a very deep level for many years.

For many years, in my prayers and research, I sought to know (1) who is really Jesus Christ? (2) Why did the apostles always baptize exclusively in the name of Jesus Christ when Jesus Himself gave them the order to baptize in the name of the Father and of the Son and of the Holy Spirit in Matthew 28:19?

These are the two questions which aroused the revelation of God in my ministry. The Lord directed me to Acts 4:12: "There is no salvation in any other; for there is no other name under heaven given among men, by which we must be saved."

The Holy Spirit, through the scriptures, began to confront us about this truth, so who really is Jesus Christ compared to what we were teaching? Like everything in its time, it was then Brother Robinette who would be the instrument that God had to use so that we had the full and correct revelation of Christ.

I came to the revelation that Lord Jesus Christ was the only name of the Father, of the Son, and of the Holy Spirit. The Lord showed me right away that the Lord Jesus Christ is the *only name* of God! For in Him, Jesus Christ our Lord dwells bodily all the fullness of the Godhead; that repentance and forgiveness of sins would be preached in His name to all nations (Col. 2: 9; Matt. 28:18; Luke 24:47).

This is a marvelous holy revelation of the absolute divinity of Christ.

As Andrew Urshan, the Pentecostal pioneer, said, "The scriptures have been revealed to my soul, as never before, by the Holy Spirit who refreshed my memory by bringing new meaning to the scriptures I had read before and they became new like the morning dew."

It is true that "the truth is progressive: when you seek God, His Spirit will guide you to a greater knowledge of his person, if you allow him."

From then on, we began to feel our consciousness (our knowledge) open more, and without delay, we began to share this testimony with other fellow pastors to whom we had the same doctrine. From then on, God united our hearts with the truth. From that point on, all across the German-speaking nations, God brought us together to reach out to many unaffiliated pastors. Many unaffiliated pastors came to the revelation of the mighty God in Christ and were rebaptized in Jesus's name and filled with the Holy Ghost.

Through the ministry of Rev. Charles G. Robinette, we have seen with our own eyes hundreds of Muslims who accepted the Gospel of salvation and, as a result, baptized by immersion in the name of Jesus Christ and receiving the Holy Ghost speaking in tongues (Acts 2:38–39).

And do you know what we found in this man, Bishop Robinette? Integrity, the fear of the Lord, a radical conservator of apostolic doctrine, a man of prayer and faith, persevering, a good steward, love of neighbor—frankly rare qualities, especially in this time of the end. One of the most important places in his ministry is the doctrine of holiness. He is someone with a spirit of humility. He knows how to trust God no matter what situation he encounters. He is not afraid or reserved to go down to Samaria if he has to go there to preach the gospel of salvation. Filled with boldness in the face of the greatest problems and he has what we call a reckless faith. He preaches with a strong and deep voice and with an attitude filled with trust in the Holy Spirit. And after preaching, he cared for people individually, and the power of God is still miraculously manifested through him. People speak in tongues, and the blind see!

The ministry of Bishop Robinette has helped me open the door to the revelation of Christ. Yes, since it was through his ministry that we received the profound revelation of the one true God, whose name is Jesus Christ, in 2016.

Rev. Naki Pedro Mumeso and Rev. Mariana Elisa Pedro Mumeso
Manage, Belgium

*****

What a tremendous honor I had to share a crusade with Rev. Robinette. We met in Peten, Guatemala, with Pastor David Bounds and the crusade team. I was excited to see how things would work out with all of us coming together for a Holy Ghost crusade. Missionary Robinette has done many crusades with thousands being filled with the Holy Ghost, and I also have been blessed to see thousands be filled with the Holy Ghost. Once again, God did the work in Peten, Guatemala. What happened through this crusade has never been seen in that area before. God filled at least 850 with the Holy Ghost, at least 60 were baptized in Jesus's name, and 358 people reported notable miracles! To God be the glory. One of the most powerful things I drew from this crusade and from teaming up with powerful men is this: when you deal with kingdom-minded and revival-driven men, no one is begging for the spotlight because there is a sense of common goals. Those goals are seeing souls be saved and letting Jesus be glorified. And look at what God did! He saved souls, and He was glorified. I want to encourage you who is reading this right now. Be a kingdom-minded and a revival-driven man or woman of God. Be willing to team up without expecting to be in the spotlight and to keep your focus on souls being saved and Jesus being glorified. Let *revival* be the name of the game.

Rev. Mark Drost
International Evangelist

*****

The ministry of Pastor Charles Robinette has profoundly impacted the New Life Family over the years. Bishop Davy first invited him to minister over fifteen years ago when his missionary career was still in its infancy.

It was at that initial meeting that we became aware of the powerful anointing that rested on his life for revival and harvest. As a church planting entity, we were constantly in need of apostolic ministry that was truly dedicated to the salvation of the lost and the expansion of the kingdom of God. Brother Robinette exemplified this in his commitment to the field in Europe and his passion for evangelism. God used his faith and zeal to facilitate explosive services where we witnessed the outpouring of the Holy Ghost, multiple water baptisms, and countless miracles.

In the last five years, we have had three crusades with him where the Lord has moved marvelously in our church family. We made the determination to have him speak at multiple church locations on Sundays in order to maximize the harvest impact of his time with us. Consequently, he would speak at the mother church in the Sunday morning service and then travel to our daughter works to preach in between services.

This redounded to the benefit of some of our church plants as they were able to experience crusade level revival services in a smaller setting. Rev. Robinette was kind enough to go beyond the call of duty in adding meetings to his already hectic schedule.

In the summer of 2014, we were privileged to see seventy-one people receive the baptism of the Holy Ghost while thirty were baptized in the name of Jesus. In the summer of 2016, there were twenty-four baptisms, and eighty received the baptism of the Holy Ghost. In 2019, we again saw over twenty-five baptized in the name of the Lord Jesus and sixty filled with the precious gift of the Spirit. Miracles, signs, and wonders accompanied the preaching of the word of God in all of these meetings. Pastor Robinette's ministry edified the church of God in a powerful way.

There is something that was particularly noteworthy in his visit to us in 2016. As the baptizer was in the pool, the presence of God hovered mightily in the baptismal area. Anyone that had not received the Holy Ghost prior to their baptism was gloriously filled as they emerged from the water. The experience had a profound impact on the minister conducting the baptisms. That same young man went on to become one of our daughter work church planters. In three years, that new church has seen over six hundred people baptized in the name of the Lord. Supernatural impartation took place in the pool as Brother Robinette ministered the Word of the Lord and operated in the gift of faith. We thank God for the prolific and anointed ministry of Rev. Charles Robinette.

Pastor Rashidi Collins
Tampa, FL

*****

In 2014, I had the blessing to get to know Pastor David and the Baptist church in Åmli, Norway. This small church, of around thirty people from the Karen state in Burma, was so hungry for God and the truth. Pastor David told me how his young people were hungry for the Holy Ghost, an experience he already had himself but had not been able to share with his youth. I told Pastor David of the ministry of Rev. Robinette and how God had used him to help people receive the Holy Ghost. We decided to invite him to Åmli.

We rented a hall close by and had his church people come to this Holy Ghost rally. We had fifteen young people from the church receive the Holy Ghost in this meeting, and after the service, we baptized them in Jesus's name. Within the following weeks, the rest of the church got rebaptized, and then joined the UPC of Norway.

Pastor David hungered to share this truth with his people in Burma and started to plan a small crusade in Pha An, Burma. This is located in the Karen State, which at this point had no apostolic churches at all. I invited Rev. Robinette with me to this first crusade. This was a door opener, and we had a great breakthrough in a small village close to Pha An. Forty-five people received the Holy Ghost, and sixteen got baptized in Jesus's name together with some great miracles.

In one of the services, a former Buddhist woman started to scream and act out as a demon bothered her. After casting out the demon, we sat her on a chair, and she instantly received the Holy Ghost. Right after church, she got baptized in Jesus's name. Right before this service, I and Rev. Robinette visited the valley of the thousand Buddhas only ten minutes from the crusade area. We prayed and took control as we proclaimed this area for the Gospel of truth.

I personally felt this incident was God showing us that the demonic power of that religion would not be able to stop the truth from being established here.

God filled another fifty with the Holy Ghost at the headquarters church in Yangon the Sunday following our crusade in Pha An. Pastor David has now established a church in that place and built a Bible school there that is educating ministers from all over the Karen State. Nine churches have been founded since this crusade. The work in the Karen State is growing with an explosive rate. The resistance is great, and some of the newly built churches have been torn down, and people are being threatened that they will be expelled from their village if they get baptized in Jesus's name. In spite of this, people are converting to the truth in a large scale.

I am so thankful for the impact Rev. Robinette has had on the work in Burma. The UPCI has a great number of people in the Chin region of Burma. They had received the apostolic message from missionaries coming over the mountain from India. Over the years, they have tried to share this with the Karen people. But it seems like they have not been so receptive, since they were the ones that brought Christianity to the Chin in the first place. But now with Pastor David being a Karen like them, they are a lot more open. Now the Chin and the Karen work side by side for this wonderful apostolic truth. The Bible school that Pastor David built is under the leadership and supervision of the headquarter Bible school in Yangon.

Pastor Goran Andreassen
Oslo, Norway

*****

Red clouds of Malawian dust swirling through the evening rays of the setting sun, white plastic chairs floating through the air, the joyous and rhythmic chanting of hundreds of people will be permanently etched into my mind. I was honored to attend the 2016

Malawi Crusade in Lilongwe. It may seem cliché, but the experience was life-changing.

Under the anointed direction of Missionary Robinette and Missionary Gibbs, the crusade team participated in a book of Acts revival accompanied by miracles, signs, and wonders. When I arrived in Malawi, I was both excited and skeptical. I was excited to be in Africa, yet I was skeptical about the stories. Could it really be as it was told? The first night changed my life. I watched as people rushed to the front to receive the Holy Ghost. As they lifted their hands and obeyed the command to shout, "Hallelujah!" they were instantly filled with the Spirit speaking with other tongues. The real demonstration and flow of the Spirit eroded all of my skepticism. The Acts of the Apostles were still alive in the twenty-first century.

But wait, that was not all. Brother Robinette came back to the pulpit and spoke to those who were not obedient or did not come forward and said, "If you did not receive the Holy Ghost, we are going to pray again."

The people who had just witnessed the operation of the supernatural but had not come forward came rushing to the front. Again at the signal, the crowd shouted, "Hallelujah!" and the Holy Ghost came rushing through the rows of people standing with their hands lifted. To my knowledge, every person who came forward and was obedient received the Holy Ghost.

That experience happened the night before the crusade began! During the crusade, I watched as smiling men and women, filled with the joy of the Lord, who walk miles for water and live on one US dollar per day, worshipped God with abandon.

There was no timekeeping, watch-looking, or boredom. The crusade was alive with the Holy Ghost! When offering time came, the people gave all they had with joy—coins, kwacha (currency), neckties, scarves, and shoes. When I came home, I began to use the same method that I saw practiced in Malawi, and I watched people receive the Holy Ghost. I witnessed people in our congregation being healed of sicknesses and diseases. Why? Because obedient, childlike faith is the antecedent to the miraculous.

Four years later, as I sit at my desk, typing these memories, my eyes fill with tears. Thank you, Brother Robinette, for allowing me to experience a modern-day outpouring of the book of Acts.

Pastor Nathan Holmes
North Little Rock, AR

A final word from Missionary Charles Robinette

We have been richly blessed during our deputations to visit so many powerful churches across North America and Canada. The UPCI has afforded us the great privilege of representing Global Missions and the vision of the organization all around the world.

We have ministered in preaching points that were in the living room of the pastor's home. We have preached in hotel conference rooms. We have carried the gospel to parks in the middle of district target cities. We have stood declaring the name of Jesus on soccer fields and in stadiums all across North America and beyond. Without a doubt, we are blessed!

During our ministry travel and deputation services in North America and Canada, we have witnessed the Lord fill over twenty-six thousand people with the Holy Ghost; over five thousand have been baptized in Jesus's name; over thirty thousand have testified of notable miracles; and God has connected our hearts with some of the most apostolic pastors, preachers, ministers, and saints, who have become such dear friends and valued prayer partners!

IN CONCLUSION

There is a concerted attempt by the enemy to distract and frustrate God's people. Distracted cannot live their divine purpose. If we are not careful, we will be at the train station of distraction when our ship of revival comes in.

Over two thousand years ago, Paul gave a detailed description of the last days, last days meaning our generation. In 2 Timothy 3, Paul itemizes nineteen societal characteristics that he summarizes as a perilous time. The characteristics are the following:

- Lovers of themselves
- Covetous
- Boasters
- Proud
- Blasphemers
- Disobedient to parents
- Unthankful
- Unholy
- Without natural affection
- Truce breakers
- False accusers
- Incontinent
- Fierce
- Despisers of those that are good
- Traitors
- Heady
- High-minded
- Lovers of pleasures more than lovers of God
- Having a form of godliness but denying the power thereof

At the conclusion of Paul's discourse, he admonishes Timothy, "From such turn away" (2 Tim. 3:5 KJV).

With all the traps in our generation, we must refuse to take the enemy's bait!

> Be sober, be vigilant; because your adversary the devil, as a roaring lion, walketh about, seeking whom he may devour: Whom resist stedfast in the faith, knowing that the same afflictions are accomplished in your brethren that are in the world. (1 Pet. 5:8–9 KJV)

A DIFFERENT KIND OF BATTLE

We do not fight like the world fights!

We, the radically apostolic church, must not allow ourselves to be drawn into the affairs of this world as political commentators, social activists, protestors, demonstrators, societal pundits, and for any worldly affair or issue!

> For though we walk in the flesh, we do not war after the flesh: (For the weapons of our warfare are not carnal, but mighty through God to the pulling down of strong holds;) Casting down imaginations, and every high thing that exalteth itself against the knowledge of God, and bringing into captivity every thought to the obedience of Christ. (2 Cor. 10:3–5 KJV)

> Jesus answered, My kingdom is not of this world: if my kingdom were of this world, then would my servants fight, that I should not be delivered to the Jews: but now is my kingdom not from hence. (John 18:36 KJV)

While the apostles and the New Testament churches were continually persecuted at the hands of an evil, lawless, and even racist society, I have not found any biblical examples where the apostles participated in rioting, demonstrating, or becoming activists in order to address any social injustices.

The Bible is clear regarding our radically apostolic role in this end-time church:

> No man that warreth entangleth himself with the affairs of this life; that he may please him who hath chosen him to be a soldier. (2 Tim. 2:4 KJV)

We should not allow ourselves to be deceived emotionally into reverting back to our old nature; fighting the way the world fights, publicly debating societal injustices on social media.

We are ministers of the gospel, not activists! We are missionaries, not politicians! We are Christians, not demonstrators!

The injustices in this present life can only be destroyed by

- faith in God (Heb. 11:1–6),
- repentance (Acts 3:19),
- baptism by emersion in Jesus's name (Rom. 6:1–6),
- being filled with the Holy Ghost with the evidence of speaking with other tongues (Acts 2:1–4, 38),
- becoming a disciple of Christ through obedience to the word of God (Jas. 1:22–25),
- through the spiritual disciplines of the effectual fervent prayer of the righteous and fasting (Jas. 5:16 and Isaiah 58:3–7), and
- taking on the holy nature of God (Heb. 12:14)!

We must never forget:

- We are called out (2 Cor. 6:17–18)!
- We are set apart (Ps. 4:3)!

- We are the light of the world and a city set on a hill (Matt. 5:14)!
- We are the salt of the earth (Matt. 5:13)!
- We are a chosen generation, royal priesthood, and holy nations (1 Pet. 2:9)!
- We are examples of the believers (1 Tim. 4:12)!
- We are ministers of the gospel of Jesus Christ (1 Cor. 4:1–2)
- We are ambassadors of Christ (2 Cor. 5:20–21)!
- We have been born again (John 3:3–7 and 1 Pet. 1:23)!
- We have a new nature (Eph. 4:22–24)!
- We have a new flag (Exod. 17:15)!
- We have a new kingdom (Matt. 6:33)!
- We are in this world, but we are not of this world (John 15:19)!

We, the radically apostolic church, must preach, teach, and live a very public example of the fruit of the Spirit mentioned in Galatians 5; while at the same time, prophetically, powerfully, and consistently praying for the kind of change in our world that will result in the salvation of 7.8 billion souls!

When I determined to write this book, I wanted to make sure that I didn't produce a clinical discourse about apostolic culture. I wanted to share my heart and illustrate each chapter with personal accounts and stories from across our fellowship. I hope I've accomplished that.

Accept the call to be *radically apostolic*!

REFERENCES

Bartleman, Frank. *How Pentecost Came to Los Angeles: As It Was in the Beginning.* Los Angeles, CA: Frank Bartleman, 1925.

———. *The Azusa Street Revival.* Revival School, 2008.

"Global Christianity: A Report on the Size and Distribution of the World's Christian Population." July 23, 2013.

Holy Bible: King James Version (KJV)

Miller, Basil. *Prayer Meetings that Made History.* Dallas: Chandler's Publications, 1955.

Murray, Andrew. *Ministry of Intercession: A Plea for More Prayer* (Updated and Annotated). S.L.: Outlook Verlag, 2016.

Pew Research Center on Religion and Public Life. December 19, 2011.

Seeking 4 Truth. https://seeking4truth.com.

Wikipedia. https://wikipedia.org.

PHOTOS

In Burma with our dear friend Pastor Gøran Andreassen, ministering to the Baptist Chin community (December 2015):

In Ethiopia with Billy Cole and the crusade team (March 2000):

In Bangladesh with our dear friends, Missionary Corbin's family, and the team (January 2020):

In Brazil with Bishop Stark and the crusade team (December 2017):

In Alaska for a North American Missions Harvest planned by our dear friend Pastor Jim Blackshear. Bro. Chris Pollard piloted me from city to city. He was such a blessing! (April 2018):

In Malawi with A-Team leader Bishop Garlitz and the crusade team (September 2007–August 2017):

In Guatemala with Pastor David Bounds and
the crusade team (April 2019):

God connected us with many unaffiliated pastors and churches. We witnessed many be baptized in Jesus's name, and they were filled with the Holy Ghost (2016–2020):

Mindanao, Philippines, Crusade with our dear
friends Bro. & Sis. Mallory (October 2019):

Many Muslims were filled with the Holy Ghost and baptized in Jesus's name in the German-speaking nations (May 2016–December 2017):

Haiti with our dear friends, Ron and Terry Brian, David and
Aimee Myers, and the team from their church (June 2018):

Thailand General Conference with Pastor Jack
Cunningham and team (January 2019):

North American Conferences:

Some of the elders that believed in and invested themselves into our ministry (Eli Hernandez, William Nix, Anthony Mangun, Jim Stark, Raymond Woodward, Lee Stoneking, Stan Gleason and Billy Cole):

My dad and mom were with us when I was ordained into the ministry:

ABOUT THE AUTHOR

Charles G. Robinette, his wife Stacey, and their two daughters Aleia and Brienna serve as United Pentecostal Church International appointed missionaries to Germany, Switzerland, Liechtenstein, and Austria.

Bro. Robinette is the general superintendent of the United Pentecostal Church of the German-speaking nations fellowship and an international evangelist, leading crusade teams across the globe.

Bro. Robinette has personally witnessed God fill over four hundred thousand people with the gift of the Holy Ghost with the evidence of speaking in other tongues. In his travels over the last two years, he has witnessed God fill at least 18,376 with the Holy Ghost, at least 5,500 were baptized in Jesus's name and over 26,723 testified of notable miracles, including blind eyes being opened, deaf ears unstopped, the lame walking, the mute speaking, creative miracles such as ears growing instantly, and all manner of diseases being miraculously healed.

The Robinettes have planted churches in Belgium, Switzerland, and Austria. They also founded the Apostolic Ministry Training Center (AMTC) in 2008. AMTC has nearly doubled in campuses, students, and instructors annually over the last four years. In 2019, during his last year as AMTC president, AMTC had thirty-one campuses and nearly five hundred students. AMTC is effectively equipping the next generation for apostolic ministry.

Bro. Robinette and his family continue to be radically apostolic!

CPSIA information can be obtained
at www.ICGtesting.com
Printed in the USA
LVHW071055100822
725627LV00008B/21/J